Luis Vidal + Architects

Expect the Unexpected

Philip Jodidio

images
Publishing

Contents

7 An Authentic Architect: The Work of Luis Vidal

15 Selected Works

16 Palmas Altas Campus

32 Private House Renovation

54 Heathrow Terminal 2

68 Can Misses Hospital

86 Álvaro Cunqueiro Hospital

110 Botín Center

126 Loyola University Campus

154 Castellana 77

164 Dallas-Fort Worth International Airport Terminal D Expansion

174 Matta Sur Community Centre & CESFAM

192 Arturo Merino Benítez International Airport Terminal 2

208 Boston Logan International Airport Terminal E Modernization

228 New Colón Towers

244 Adolfo Suárez Madrid-Barajas Airport T4 & T4S Expansion and Modernization

254 Projects for the Future

Appendix

258 Selected Awards and Achievements for Featured Projects

260 Complete List of Works

266 Team

270 Image Credits

271 Acknowledgments

An Authentic Architect
The Work of Luis Vidal

In a relatively short period of time, Luis Vidal has built airports and other buildings around the world, on schedule and on budget. He has done this in large part by remaining authentic in his choices of materials, forms spaces inhabited by light, and not ceding to the sirens of artificial form and artistic ambition. He has done this by carefully controlling every aspect of what makes a building work.

Born in 1969 in Barcelona, Luis Vidal was led early in his life to explore the possibilities offered by other countries. Partially raised in Mallorca, he did A-level studies at an English school there before earning his BA in Architecture at Thames Polytechnic (RIBA I, London, 1991). This was followed by a Diploma in Architecture specializing in airports, offices, residential, and museums from the University of Greenwich (RIBA II, London, 1994) and finally a Postgraduate Certificate in Professional Architectural Studies from the same institution (RIBA III, 1995). Vidal explains that even by the time he was well into his architecture studies, "I had never been to Madrid—it is like being from Manchester and never going to London. I came to visit a friend and met my future wife Patricia Rojas then. We started working in London and then I got a job offer in Madrid."

Up, Up, and Away

He started as an architect in the Madrid practice Estudio Lamela in 1994 and began a very rapid rise in responsibility that led him to play a key role in what remains one of his most emblematic projects—the design and construction of Terminal 4 at the Adolfo Suárez Madrid-Barajas Airport. By that time, he had been promoted to Senior Project Architect in the firm (1995), Senior Projects Director (1996) and Managing Director (1997). The competition for T4 and T4S the satellite facility was launched in 1997. He explains, "I was working at Estudio Lamela, and I was twenty-eight years old when I managed to convince Richard Rogers to work with me on the project; and we won the competition. I just went to knock on his door. When Richard said he wanted me to be the project director, I was so honored."

The T4 expansion was no small matter. Designed by Richard Rogers Partnership (now RSHP/Rogers Stirk Harbor + Partners) with Estudio Lamela between 1997 and 1999, it was built between 2000 (when Vidal became a partner in Estudio Lamela) and 2005. With a budget of €1 billion, the facility includes the T4 terminal itself (470,000 square meters [5,059,038 square feet]), the T4S satellite (315,000 square meters [3,390,632 square feet]) and a parking facility (370,000 square meters [3,982,647 square feet]), making it the largest terminal in Spain. The structural engineer for the competition phase was Anthony Hunt, celebrated for his work with Rogers, but also with Norman Foster, Nicholas Grimshaw, and others. In this prestigious company, the young Luis Vidal left his mark in no uncertain way, displaying a practical sense and a determination that resolved potentially difficult practical and aesthetic problems.

Some of the signature features of T4 are its wave-like roof, and the materials used for the interior. When asked how the wave form was created, Vidal responds, "It was a question of making the building integrate into the landscape. The main terminal is 1.1 kilometers (0.68 miles) long. The satellite is 950 meters (3,117 feet) long. It is huge. We were very concerned that the building would stand out too much from its environment. We sank the building down as much as we could and then we tried to emulate the hilly surroundings. The wavy roof came from trying to make it look as natural and as low as possible. The project was on a short schedule and a low budget. The entire project is based on a 9-meter (29.5-foot) module that is repeated throughout—it is extruded and extended everywhere. We designed the roof in common with Richard in London, when we prepared the competition and developed the design."

A Material Palette

Visitors today to the Barajas T4 will note the light, airy feeling of the interior spaces. Aside from ample natural light, the terminal has an uplifting feeling that escapes most modern airports. This is due in part to a careful choice of materials. Vidal continues, "We proposed a bamboo ceiling and the contractor naturally tried to do it with printed aluminum. I went to many places that produce bamboo—from Ecuador to China—until we sorted it out, and T4 was built with real bamboo. We wanted a sustainable material, and the amount of bamboo we used grew back in just six months. Another reason for the final selection of bamboo was that it can take double curvature, which aluminum cannot. We faced another hurdle with the flooring, which we chose to be a light, cream-colored Mistral Spanish limestone. Suppliers applied huge pressure to use gray granite—the Berroqueña stone that both the Prado and El Escorial were built in. But the T4 project is about natural light, the warmth and texture of the materials; gray granite would not have been the right choice."[1]

Flying Solo

As work on Barajas was finishing, and Vidal had already proven his capacity to deal with large-scale projects, he decided to create his own firm. "When I decided to go solo," he explains, "Richard offered that I become a partner in his practice, but I felt that I needed to be independent. He said we could use each other's office; my office in Spain would be shared and I could decide what we would do together. He was always incredibly generous with me." He founded Luis Vidal + Architects in Madrid in 2004. Several prestigious projects followed, and Vidal confirmed his emerging position as one of the leading airport designers with the commission to design Heathrow Airport Terminal 2 (London, 2008–2014). With an area of 220,000 square meters (2,368,060 square feet), this five-story building with a 522-meter-long (1,712.5-foot-long) satellite pier (T2B, designed and built by Grimshaw Architects prior to Vidal starting T2A) was the first airport in the world to obtain a BREEAM Excellent rating. This and other designs confirmed his capacity to deliver major projects on schedule and on budget. A waved roof covering 54,000 square meters (581,251 square feet) marks the facility as does the ample natural light. In 2018, Heathrow T2, which was phased into operation for twenty-six airlines in 2014, was selected as the Best Airport Terminal in the World by Skytrax. Clearly, Luis Vidal's studies in the United Kingdom and partnership with English architects and engineers made work on T2 possible for him and established his firm as an international practice almost immediately after its creation.

Compression and Expansion

At the time he was working on Heathrow, Luis Vidal undertook a much smaller, but in a sense equally important, project for a private house in the Puerta de Hierro area of Madrid. It is quite intentional that he places this house near the beginning of this volume, precisely because it includes much of the thinking that has made his work so successful across the world, while also being an intensely personal endeavor. It is a process that is best explained in his own words.

---

1 Luis Vidal in conversation with the author, Madrid, September 27, 2023. This quotation and others in this essay are all from this conversation, unless stated otherwise.

Can you tell me more about the private house, as it includes many of the architectural ideas that were later applied to other projects at a larger scale.

Luis Vidal The house was built around 1965. It was redone in two phases. Phase 1 was in 2007, and Phase 2 was completed in 2011. It was originally a two-story brick residence with load-bearing walls, a basement, a small garage, a ground floor, and a modest upper level with a pitched roof. We started by digging a 200-meter-deep (656-foot-deep) geothermal well, making this only the second private home in Madrid to use geothermal energy. We decided on radiant floor heating. We stripped out the walls and the small windows, creating full-height openings. The perimeter of the ground floor of the new house is similar in size, but we have completely connected the interior and the exterior. This is a feature that exists in many of our buildings. In the kitchen we kept the original ceiling height and floor cladding, creating a lasting rapport with the earlier architecture. The new design relies on natural cross-ventilation and convection—air conditioning is not necessary. The geothermal system cools the floor in summer and heats it in winter. We designed Phase 2 of the project between 2009 and 2011 and then construction work started. That involved removing the top level of the existing house, and adding porticos that bridge over the old house. We created three new floors and extended a bit, including the garage, which now has space for several cars. We also replanted the garden with fruit trees and created a pool just outside the living area. We kept the palm trees that had been planted by the previous owners in 1965. In fact, saving the palm trees was a driving force in the final form of the house and its design.

You employed an industrial vocabulary for some of the metal surfaces, including the aluminum forms used for the ceilings?

Luis Vidal Absolutely. The ceilings are made with aluminum forms that are used to pour concrete. The original material is anodized, but we painted it. The use of industrial materials in residential architecture remains very rare in Spain, it is more frequent in the United States, for example. I wanted to express the structure.

The stones and colors you used are directly related to your work on airports for example.

Luis Vidal I am very interested in colors, such as the rainbow used at Barajas and the red employed in Boston. For the house, we had so many samples of colors—we came in during the day, at night. We decided on a silver color after trying purple, violet, blue, green, and other shades. The house was designed and built roughly in parallel with our Heathrow Terminal 2, so there are lots of things that were imagined here and then used at Heathrow. We have large blocks of natural stone on the floors. This comes from Terminal 4 in Madrid, I tried to bring large-scale stones into that terminal. It was my thought that when stone is quarried, it is usually cut into much smaller surfaces. Why do that? Today we have technology to move big weights, and it is possible to avoid all the cutting. In T4, I was not able to use this system, but in this house, I could, and was using 1.8-meter-long (5.9-foot-long) pieces of naturally black granite. We designed the tables, chairs, sofas, the Corten steel chimney. This house was conceived like a pavilion, where you are outside and inside at the same time. The windows are all operable. The spaces connect between each other, visually or spatially. This house is the seed of most of our projects. The apparently white façades of the house were finished with prismatic paint that changes its tone according to lighting conditions and angle of view. It has a pearl shade, but it can become greener, or violet depending on the time of the day. We developed this kind of prismatic paint for Vigo and for Boston.

The house reveals its underlying connections to other work undertaken by Luis Vidal in its name but also in many other details. It is dubbed T8 because, as Vidal explains, "The name of the street here starts with a T, and we call the house T8, so we have done T2 in London, T4 in

Madrid, and here, T8." The architect goes on to state, "I selected the granite of the pool when we did the Zaragoza Airport at the time of the Expo in 2008, which was about "Water and Sustainable Development." I picked the stone because it reminded me of water on the shore as it moves." With no precise front door, instead several different entries, T8 is most readily approached through a narrow passage fashioned in Corten steel. He explains, "A lot of our buildings are about compression and expansion. The passage leading up to the house along the outside, lined in Corten steel is compressed." The balustrade and bespoke chimney of the house are also in Corten, giving a material continuity that transitions from the exterior to the interior areas, including the garden. The "expansion" that Vidal refers to is readily apparent in the main volumes of the house. "We wanted the spaces to connect, to allow for views and even sounds to travel through the house from every angle." Another revealing aspect of the house is that Luis Vidal did not want to simply erase the past, in the form of the house that was on this site. Instead, he built over and around it. "I wanted the porticos that bridge over the old house to be legible, that is why you can see the black columns and the beams," he says.

In a time when slick cladding can easily disguise the workings of a building, Vidal's gesture here, in exposing the columns and beams, is an indication of his close attachment to the realities of architecture—what makes things hold up and function correctly, even in a climate given to temperature extremes like that of Madrid. His participation in the final appearance of the house extends to some of the furnishings, although his object designs are relatively infrequent. "I designed a table," says the architect. "You can never fit more than six people at a table and have a proper conversation—with tables of eight or ten there are always two conversations. Why can't we design a table where more people can come close together? It is curved, a little like a clover leaf. It was also designed to allow for more than one table to be fit together with other ones. I did a series of twenty of them with my team, which are all numbered and signed. I call it the Clover table. I have not designed much other furniture, but with Richard, we did the ceiling lights for T4."

Red like Boston

The interest of Luis Vidal in what might be called "signature" colors, such as the "prismatic" red employed for the Boston Logan International Airport Terminal E project (2017–2023) is more than anecdotal, and it does express a quality that is not necessarily shared to this degree by other significant architects. Why red for Boston Logan? Luis Vidal explains:

> Every time I am going to build in a new city, I try to absorb as much as I can of the local culture and society. I literally move for a certain time into that city. I went to Pittsburgh in each of the four seasons. I had been visiting Boston since 2012. One of the things I always noticed there was the quality of the light. It reminded me a bit of the light of Madrid—beautiful sunsets and mornings. It can also be gray and windy. The color of the traditional buildings—all that brick. The fall foliage in the park. Many of the local institutions such as Harvard, MIT, or the Boston Red Sox. The airport has a view of the Boston skyline, and a red sunset was what convinced me that the new building should be red. But then I said to myself that we had to design a red, we couldn't just use Ferrari red or cherry red—it had to be a special color that is dynamic and not static. I imagined a dynamic building that would change almost instantly as the light changes. I had designed a changing blue for Vigo with Monopol and I went there, in the Canton of Aargau in Switzerland, and spent three days designing this red. For a prismatic paint, you have a base color—which can be any color, white, green blue—then you apply a layer of mixed colors with powdered glass; the possible combinations are infinite. With a prismatic paint, as the light comes in, it bounces off the glass powder and the base colors and comes out again. The glass breaks light into its seven constituent colors and can thus generate literally millions of possible combinations. This is done manually through a trial-and-error process. I finally found a red combination, with yellow, orange, gold, and burgundy. I went with a sample to the client. And his first question was: How much extra would this cost? I told him it was less than $1 extra for every

10 square meters (108 square feet) to be painted. The lifespan of the color is as good as any other of the finest paints. It doesn't fade. They agreed but asked why not green or blue—and we tried those, too. We did a video called Boston Red that I presented to the mayor. He liked it so much he asked to use it himself.

I Did it My Way

Luis Vidal has established himself as one of the leading airport designers in the world, a fact that brings to mind at least one other architect who previously dominated the field, the Frenchman Paul Andreu (1938–2018). Chief Architect of Aéroports de Paris, he developed the Roissy Charles-de-Gaulle site as well as many international hubs across the world. Vidal accepts the comparison to a certain extent, saying, "I am different from Paul Andreu, but he was one of the airport designers I admire most. The difference with us is that Aéroports de Paris is majority-owned by the French government. A lot of the work Andreu came through the French government. He designed about eighty-five airports—we have done thirty, and I still have some years to go. In each case, we work with the best available consultants—our designs are as good as the teams we put together. We are an entirely private practice, and we must fight for everything we do. It is also about trust. None of our buildings have ever been over cost or over schedule. Heathrow had an £880 million budget and we delivered for £800 million. We saved £80 million for the client. That is very rare!"

Back to Barajas

An indication of the veracity of Vidal's statements can readily be found in one of his current projects, the expansion, remodeling, and demolition at the Adolfo Suárez Madrid-Barajas Airport, where he worked at the beginning of the twenty-first century with Richard Rogers. In this case, his firm won an open, public competition (with the engineers TYPSA) to design new facilities related to T4 that encompass 270,738 square meters (2,914,200 square feet) of expansion; 63,374 square meters (682,152 square feet) of remodeling; and 5,888 square meters (63,378 square feet) of demolition for a budget of €1.6 billion. Luis Vidal explains "Our project, developed between 2021 and 2023, set the basis for the design and execution of the T4 and T4S expansion, remodeling, and necessary demolition for the expansion and remodeling. It was not straightforward, as we worked very hard to keep the essence of the 1997 design idea, but having to work with new building codes, new materials (some are not available anymore), construction technologies (please note this is twenty-two years later, from 1997 to 2019)." Luis Vidal remained close to Richard Rogers (d. 2021) until the end of his life and was eager to share his ideas for the project. "In one of my last conversations with Richard Rogers, he told me that he was very happy that we won this competition for the airport, which originally brought us together; he said, 'Better you than anyone else.' I also traveled to London to explain my new theory to him on how the colors on the steel columns could be extended. The color scheme, which had been likened to a 'rainbow'—red/hot South, blue/cold North—was one of my contributions to the original buildings. We have now completed the necessary concept and design elements that make it possible for others to continue our work and produce working drawings in 2023."[2]

Between Richard and Renzo

The relationship between Richard Rogers and Luis Vidal had one other important consequence in the form of Vidal's participation as "co-architect" with Renzo Piano (RPBW) in the Botín Art and Culture Center (Santander, 2011–2017). This 10,000-square-meter (107,639-square-foot) building that rises at the water's edge is a prestigious space devoted to the ongoing work of the Fundación Botín, and in particular that of Emilio Botín (1934–2014), the former head of Banco Santander and long-time President of the Foundation. Luis Vidal explains, "Renzo Piano was approached by Emilio Botín for the Botín Center in Santander. They took a boat

---

2   Luis Vidal, e-mail to the author, October 29, 2023.

and sailed around the bay and Renzo eventually accepted. He needed a Spanish partner. I have become weary of the expression 'local architect'—we are not a technical practice or an 'architect of record' as they say in the United States, we are not the type of firm that just signs plans. We believe that we can add value from the beginning. Renzo Piano spoke to Richard Rogers about the project and the need for a Spanish partner to participate. Richard told him not to hesitate, but to go with me. This was just a phone call between them. The client was not involved; Piano called and invited me to do this project with him." It is certainly interesting that Luis Vidal had the idea to "just knock on the door" to meet Rogers and participate with him in the Madrid Barajas, and that that contact, which developed into a long-term friendship still had direct consequences fifteen years after the fact.

LEED and BREEAM

Although he emphasizes that most of his firm's projects come through competitions, after revealing the source of his involvement in the Botín Center, he states, "We also have private clients. We have the towers in the Plaza Colón in Madrid. The client came to us and asked us to carry out projects without any competition. For the Loyola University in Seville, we came into a limited competition and told the client that the budget they were proposing was actually 20 percent higher than necessary—this and the quality of our project are why we were selected."

The New Colón Towers project involves an iconic twin tower designed in 1968 and completed in 1976 by the architect Antonio Lamela and updated in 1992 by Antonio and his son Carlos— of the firm with that Vidal began his career in 1994. The new Vidal design for the Colón Towers (2019–ongoing) integrates energy-efficient solutions, including a cogeneration energy system, a new façade that greatly improves acoustics and insulation, and elevators will have energy recovery units. The Loyola University Campus involved a first project carried out in 2013–2019, which received the first LEED Platinum certification for a project of its type in the world. A second phase has recently been successfully completed. Although Spanish legislation is not among the most stringent in terms of sustainability and energy use in construction, Luis Vidal has taken a lead in this domain, convinced that architecture has a significant role to play in the current environmental situation. This approach was also demonstrated clearly in his renovation of Castellana 77 (2015–2017), an eighteen-story tower in Madrid originally built in 1977. The completed project won another LEED Platinum certification for its innovative use of an EFTE skin and slats that control solar gain, among other ecologically oriented aspects.

Although their function is radically different than that of airports, hospital design is also very demanding in terms of technical requirements and flexibility to accommodate rapid changes in health care. Luis Vidal has also excelled in this very specific sector of contemporary architecture, using elements such as intuitive wayfinding, natural life and vegetation, as he has also done in airports. The Álvaro Cunqueiro Hospital in Vigo (2011–2015) was built to serve a local population of 600,000. Sunlit spaces and a therapeutic garden are among the added design elements that make a visit to the hospital less stressful than it might be elsewhere. Outpatient facilities are in the lower part of the hilltop hospital, below a garden and public space that provides access to the main hospitalization area that is divided into six blocks overlooking the neighboring landscape. Energy efficiency and sustainability were significant elements in this project. Passive strategies were used together with a photovoltaic plant, a thermal plant with biomass boilers, and LED lighting with automated control systems. Cooling using naturally cool air or water instead of mechanical refrigeration is employed together with air conditioning and chillers that rely on energy recovery. The overall energy scheme allowed the project to become the first hospital to receive BREEAM certification and was used as a benchmark case for subsequent BREEAM hospitals. Vidal also created a very specific shade of blue prismatic paint again with the Swiss firm Monopol for this project—the shades and nuances of the color change as they are viewed at different times of the day, or from different angles.

Vidal's Can Misses Hospital (Ibiza, 2008–2014) involved the refurbishment and extension of an existing public health facility, tripling the medical areas and updating patterns of staff work through the architectural design. The architect used white as the predominant shade of the building, making it blend into the island's buildings, but also used stripes of photoluminescent paint to make the structure glow slightly after dark so that it would be readily identifiable. The careful design preparation allowed the hospital to continue to function throughout the construction, a significant fact since it is the only public health care facility on the islands of Ibiza and Formentera. Continuity of function has also been a hallmark of Vidal's airport projects.

Functional and Pragmatic

Perhaps because he engaged almost immediately in large-scale architectural projects like airports that have their own functional design imperatives, it may appear that Luis Vidal does not necessarily have a recognizable style in his work. In fact, this is true of many of the major architects working in the world today—there has been a shift from purely aesthetic or "artistic" design to architecture that is more focused on the specifics of a given project—its location, function, and ambitions in terms of visibility. Vidal has shown a mastery of all the moving parts that go together to make a complex building work. In fact, he is a collector of vintage automobiles and says, "The way the mechanics work, how everything is put together, is very much like architecture, a kit of parts where things have to work together." But there are other characteristic elements in his design that he readily explains:

> What is Vidal's style? Of course, you can identify buildings by Gehry or Calatrava. If you think of less well-known architects, you may mistakenly identify people who are trying to copy others. Our style? We always put the user first. Our language involves intuitive wayfinding, the use of natural light and ventilation, and of color. The expressivity of the materials and our deep commitment to function and then whatever makes the form. We always work first on the function. This generates different building forms obviously and means that there may not be a recognizable style.

This lack of a recognizable style but also the very visible success of Luis Vidal may also be due to the emphasis that he places on efficiency and knowing just how a building will function and age. He says quite simply, "I am functional and pragmatic. I am worried that a building won't leak, which is a technical issue. I am as concerned that the paint won't fade with the sun. I am very practically inclined which makes me put my hands on anything that makes the building work." Then, too, the type of large structures that Vidal has worked on extensively—airports and hospitals notably—rely on budgetary constraints and the need for flexibility and potential expansion in the future. These characteristics imply certain types of design. Luis Vidal confirms, "We do look for modularity, which results in savings because it facilitates prefabrication and gives flexibility. We always see how our buildings can grow or change with time. Airports obviously expand, but hospitals need to be able to change to keep up with changes in medicine. You need to be able to readily change the allocation of space."

Although his firm carries his name, and Luis Vidal expresses his opinions and architectural ideas freely, he is also quick to explain that the success of his office relies on his own relationship with a larger team that understands and amplifies his way of working.

> With the exception of Botín, we have earned most of our projects alone. We fight on our own—it is me, but it is my team; I think we have the best team in the world. Some come from my previous practice, some were my students, others came through the hiring process. We are at the forefront of highly technological design using AI, big data, Virtual reality (VR), which may already be of the past. I remain very much hands-on. We put the designs on paper, hang them on the wall, and have open discussions about them. This can apply to color samples, functional layouts, or constructability issues. Computers help us to speed up the options process. We still rely on our instinct and our experience. We have the connection with the client, we know the industry, we know what a contractor can do. We have built in the Dominican Republic, and in Boston, and that represents a huge difference in the capabilities of contractors. You need to understand what you can propose anywhere you work.

In a period when computers have taken center stage, Luis Vidal works in many ways as he always has: starting with sketches and in close collaboration with his team. What has changed of course, is the way his sketches and concepts are translated into options that are used to further investigate possible design solutions. Working closely not only with his team but with clients, these concepts are then translated into the completed buildings. He says, "I sketch all the time. The last thing I did before I left the office yesterday had to do with the LAX Terminal 9 competition—I spent two hours sketching. When I return to the office, I share these sketches with the team. I enjoy being at the forefront of the project—from the conceptual input, and throughout the evolution of the designs."

Mies, Ando, and a Ray of Light

Another way of appreciating the direction and approach of Luis Vidal is to enquire about the architects or the buildings he most admires. In this instance he moves rapidly from a few names to very practical issues of natural light, solar gain, and how buildings can best be used:

> A number of architects have influenced my life—my mentor was Richard Rogers. I learned from him on both the personal and professional levels. I always like Mies van der Rohe, Tadao Ando, people who are authentic in expressing their way of building or their materials. When you look at Spanish architecture—we don't have many big names. I think of Grand Central Terminal in New York—I am fascinated by the light there, and I also admire the work of Louis I. Kahn who was a master of light. I believe that we build with the cheapest possible building material, which is natural light. That is always one of our starting points. You don't want too much nor too little—you don't want too much solar gain. Football stadiums are used once every two weeks or so, hospitals operate 24/7, so depending on function and location, the needs for light are clearly different. This also applies to access and many other important issues. Since football stadiums are usually well located, there is a realization that there is a need to maximize or certainly increase their use all year round.

The words of Luis Vidal reproduced here were mostly spoken in the house that he chose to put forward in this book. In this house, he built over and beyond an existing residence, adding powerful, contemporary spaces in a way that shows their architectural authenticity—there is no pretense here, no artificiality—what you see is what you get. But then, you see more than you would in any ordinary house—the light, the materials, and the spaces were crafted by an architect who has thought about how glass, granite, Corten steel, and a garden can create a sheltered home that is also open to the world.

Modern materials and computer-driven designs have made it possible to create almost any aesthetic fantasy, what remains a task for architects like Luis Vidal is to be authentic in the choice of materials, forms, and spaces, to privilege function and the user. To remain connected to what architecture is really about, even at the scale of a major international airport.

Philip Jodidio
Lausanne, Switzerland
November 2023

Selected Works

Client: Abengoa
Architects: Luis Vidal + Architects in association
with Rogers Stirk Harbour + Partners (RSHP)
Area: 100,000 m² (1,076,391 ft²)
Budget: €100 million
Certification: LEED Platinum

Seville, Spain

Palmas Altas Campus

2005–2009

The Palmas Altas technology center was designed with co-architects Rogers Stirk Harbour + Partners (RSHP) to create a "benchmark" in sustainable architecture, an objective that was achieved when the campus obtained a LEED Platinum certification in 2015. The complex includes seven buildings, five of which were occupied by the corporation Abengoa, and the remaining two by tenants who have synergies with the client. Abengoa is an international company that "applies innovative technology solutions for sustainability in the infrastructures, energy, and water sectors."

The buildings provide about 47,000 square meters (505,904 square feet) of office space in self-contained structures that are three or four levels in height. The buildings are arranged on either side of a central space forming a sequence of interconnected plazas. This is a project that goes beyond the typical characteristics of a business park: it becomes an authentic compact community, grouped around a square. The design offers spaces that have a strong sense of cohesion and encourage interaction and collaboration between workers. Likewise, the scale of the buildings ensures the quality of life of its users by providing natural ventilation and natural light throughout the interior, with slats on the façades that control excessive light and solar gain.

In each building, the spaces are connected vertically on the outside through an atrium that acts as a unifying central courtyard. The project integrates state-of-the-art environmental technologies, such as photovoltaic panels, a trigeneration plant, hydrogen batteries, and efficient air-conditioning and lighting systems. Energy-saving criteria are also applied in all aspects of the design: from the geometry of the building, which is based on compact forms, to the composition of the building envelope, the distribution and design of solar control devices, and the choice of materials. The plan considers the location of the buildings so that they respectively shade their own east and west façades.

The result is an innovative design, intended exclusively for pedestrian use, which is likely to become a standard for the office typology of the future. The complex received a 2010 RIBA European Award.

Inspired by the courtyards in the Andalusian vernacular architecture, this energy-efficient business park consists of a series of self-shading, compact building blocks. They are distributed along an axis that articulates the common areas in which water features, sunken courtyards, and green areas regulate the high temperatures in the Seville summer.

Expect the Unexpected 21

Palmas Altas Campus

Expect the Unexpected 25

Palmas Altas Campus

Expect the Unexpected 27

Palmas Altas Campus

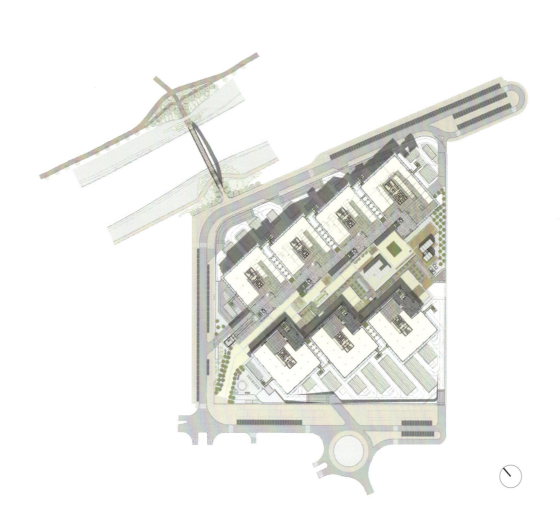

Area: 950 m² (10,226 ft²)
Status: Built

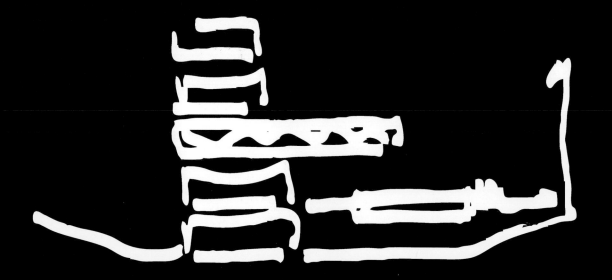

Madrid, Spain

Private House Renovation

2007 (Phase 1); 2009–2011 (Phase 2)

This project was a renovation of a traditional late 1960s three-story house located in Madrid's residential area of Puerta de Hierro. After an in-depth study, the residence was freed of its original closed design, privileging a new sense of clarity and openness. Connecting the interiors with the garden and swimming pool was a priority of the intervention. Large windows were created, perforating the façade, and allowing uninterrupted views of the gardens and surrounding trees. A horizontal plan was developed, with a continuous black stone surface, both inside and around the exterior.

The house occupies 30 percent of the site, fully dissolving barriers between the more sheltered living space and the gardens. Described by visitors as a "pavilion in the middle of the woods," the house is set on a sloped site between two parallel residential streets.

Palm trees planted in 1965 were preserved during construction, which was carried out in two phases. During the first phase, in 2007, a geothermal well was drilled and internal walls that had divided the living space were removed. Small windows with protective bars were replaced by full-height glazing and it was decided not to have a main entrance as such. A ground-floor pavilion was converted to create bedrooms for the family's three children. In the second phase of renovation, carried out between 2009 and 2011, most of the original roof was removed and two new floors were added. The garage and ground floor were extended, the existing swimming pool was enlarged, and a lap pool was added on the second level near the master bedroom. Corten steel was used for a new chimney, fence, and balustrade. Stone paving included green Verde Coto granite for the exteriors and the pool. According to the architect, "natural light is the main material that connects all spaces. With added openings in the form of skylights, all levels are flooded with natural light." A paint similar to that used for "stealth" aircraft was chosen for the exterior unrendered concrete walls.

The same attention to detail given to private residences is given to all projects the firm works on. The well-being of users is at the core of all design decisions, extending the sense of comfort of a home to a diversity of typologies, including hospitals, airports, and community centers.

Furniture, as an extension of the body and a mediated object for comfort, is a key design element of the firm's holistic approach. Clover table was originally designed as a reflective surface held by an undulating metal strap inspired by the flexibility of natural leather. Its shape radically redefines the relational nature of dining by bringing people closer together.

RS (Reina Sofía) chair was originally designed for the restaurant and café at the Reina Sofía Museum in Madrid. It was then commercialized, and Viccarbe presented it at the 2006 Milan Furniture Fair as a stackable, functional design upholstered with a low-maintenance textile. This chair design was soon joined by other pieces that allowed flexibility of use in different internal environments. This included the T sofa, a sofa bed with an integrated working station, and the M sofa, also known as the Step sofa, a modular stackable system that enables any interior to perform as a seated amphitheater.

A lover of the sea, Luis Vidal often puts emphasis on water reflections and the diffractions that architectural materials bring into interiors as a technique to blur the physical boundary between inside and outside. The pool of water in this residence is encased with Verde Coto stone slabs from the same quarry as the ones used in the terminal building for Zaragoza Airport. The pattern in the stone resembles the sun glittering over the shore.

In the building refurbishments that the firm undertakes, there is often an element that anchors the new design to the original historical fabric. These palm trees planted by the previous house owner embody the first gesture of nesting in their new home. As part of the bold architectural gestures that followed, the team designed vertical circulation around the palm trees that visually and physically connects different private spaces of the house. Bridging past and future, while sustainably innovating radical transformation, is at the core of the firm's designs.

This spread: Further dissolving the barriers between indoors and outdoors, skylights were placed over every bed in the house, allowing a view and connection with the sky.

Expect the Unexpected 51

Private Home Renovation

Following spread: The house appears to float, giving the illusion that the outside extends all the way inside, and inside is also part of outside, blending both into one space.

Client: HETCo (joint venture between Ferrovial Construction
and Laing O´Rourke)
Area: 220,000 m² (2,368,060 ft²)
Budget: £880 million
Capacity: 20 million passengers/year
Status: Built
Certification: BREEAM Excellent

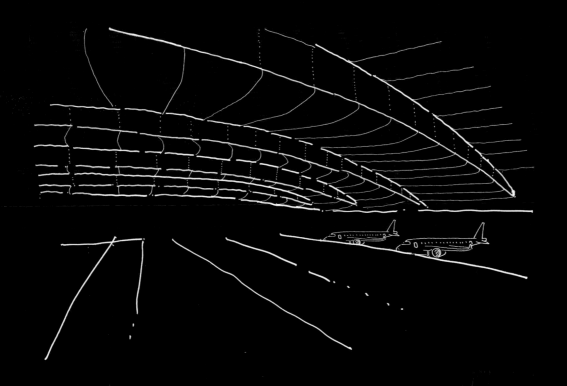

London, United Kingdom

Heathrow Terminal 2

2008–2014

Terminal 2 (T2) at Heathrow Airport, called The Queen's Terminal, is the world's first airport to obtain a BREEAM Excellent rating, thanks to a design conceived to reduce CO_2 emissions by 40 percent through a combination of active and passive systems. Apart from making use of 1,000 square meters (10,764 square feet) of photovoltaic panels on its canopy, T2 has a wood-fired combined heat- and power-generating facility comprising highly efficient gas boilers and a cooling center. Located at the heart of Heathrow, T2 is centered on a five-story main building (T2A and a 522-meter-long (1,712.5-foot-long) satellite pier called Terminal T2B designed by Grimshaw Architects prior to Luis Vidal + Architects' design for Terminal T2A). A four-story car park for 1,300 vehicles is also part of the scheme.

The original T2, Heathrow's oldest passenger terminal operating since 1955, was closed in November 2009 and demolished a year later to enable the construction of the new terminal T2A. Most of the material derived from the demolition was either recycled or reused. Foster + Partners were the Heathrow Airport master planners and the East terminal building concept architects during the initial project phase. The project used a construction method that minimized the impact on the facilities and the adjacent urban and airport environment, a goal achieved through innovative solutions based on a modular system and a carefully planned construction schedule. The Queen's Terminal was inaugurated by Queen Elizabeth II on June 23, 2014, and opened in a phased manner with twenty-six airlines moving into the terminal over a six-month period in 2014. Terminal 2 is Phase 1 of a three-phase master plan also developed by Luis Vidal + Architects. Phase 1 is this project (20 million passengers/year) + Phase 2 (10 million passengers/year) + Phase 3 (10 million passengers/year), for a total 40 million passengers/year.

The Queen's Terminal develops under a 54,000-square-meter (581,251-square-foot) roof whose three large waves emphasize the three main parts of the process passengers go through when flying: check-in, security control, and departure. Thus, function and form are integrated and help passenger intuitive orientation. The waves of the roof are tilted against each other, housing skylights in their intersections, all facing north to allow for ample natural light, while reducing solar gain and contributing energy savings. Departing passengers enjoy more than 20,000 square meters (215,278 square feet) of retail areas offering excellent views of the flight field, and which are distributed on two floors, next to the boarding gates. An unusual feature of the building is a monumental sculpture by the United Kingdom–based artist Richard Wilson called *Slipstream*. At over 70 meters (230 feet) in length, the work is suspended between two passenger walkways and was inspired by the flight pattern of a stunt plane.

In 2018, Heathrow T2 was selected as the World's Best Airport Terminal by Skytrax. It also received a Green Good Design® Award, which was one of more than twenty-seven international awards and nominations for the terminal. The evaluation of the building from the Green Good Design® Awards read in part, "Terminal 2A has been designed to be as energy efficient as possible. In addition to the use of natural light, there are large overhangs to provide shading on the east and west façades, so minimizing solar gain. On the south façade there is a brise-soleil consisting of aluminum solid tubes and metallic louvers."

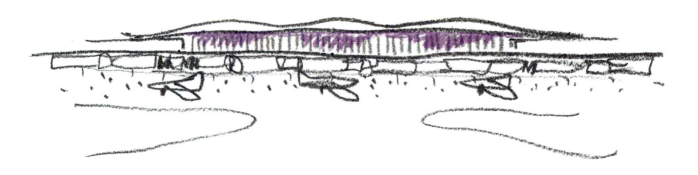

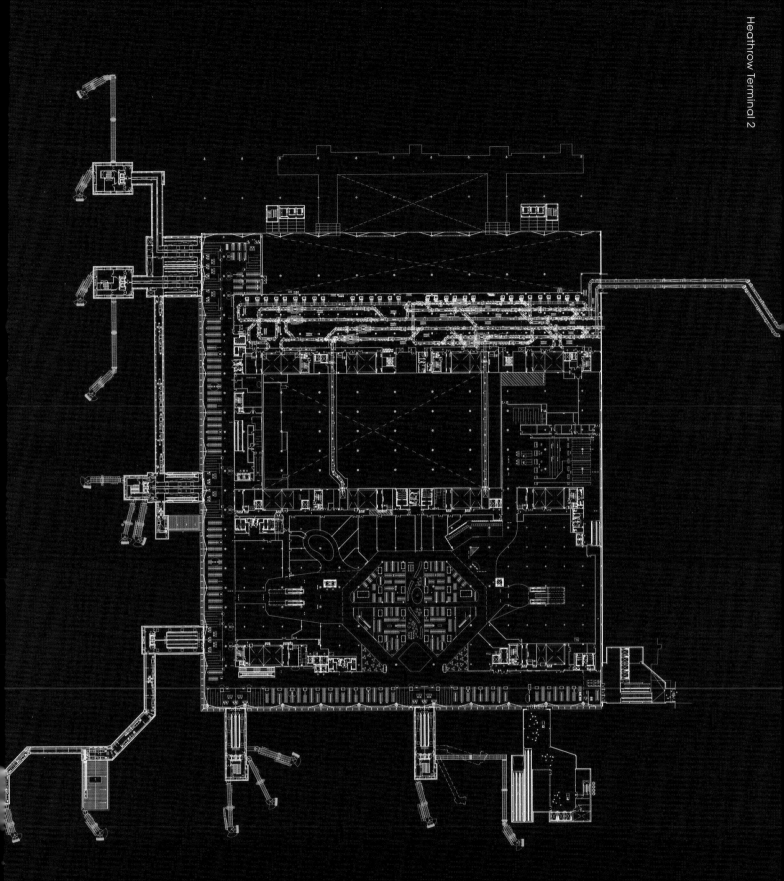

"Spaces should be made beautiful. Give them the right light, the right exposure, texture and color, the right sound, the right height. Architecture not only must observe this matter, but also the void."

—Luis Vidal

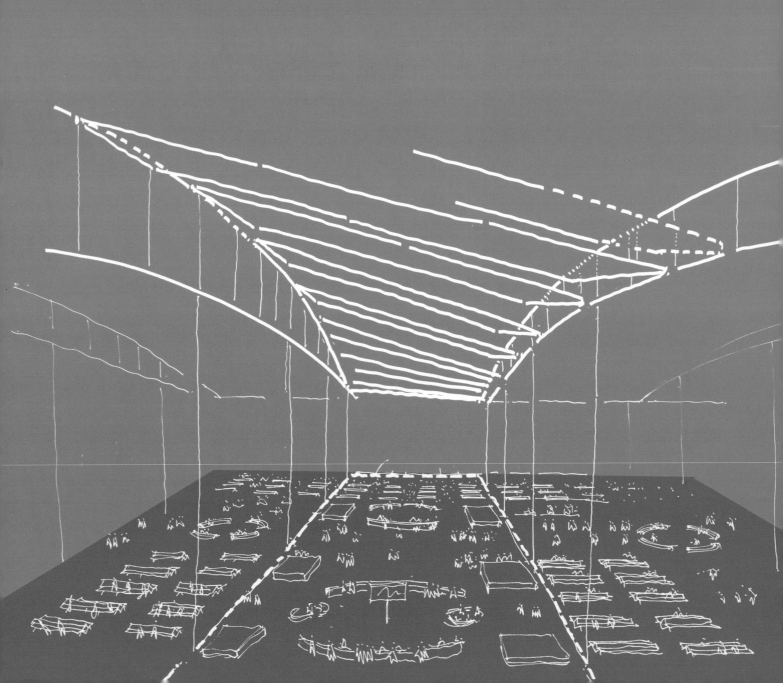

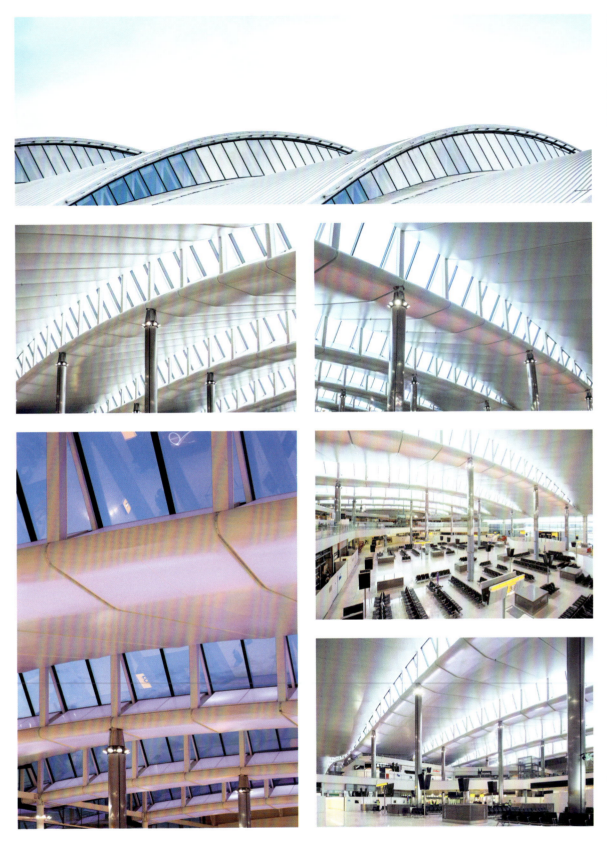

The lighting strategy sought to bring a changing visual effect to internal surfaces. This interest in exploring surfaces that subtly change color depending on the viewer's position and the lighting conditions was the precursor for the search of materials, such as the prismatic paint.

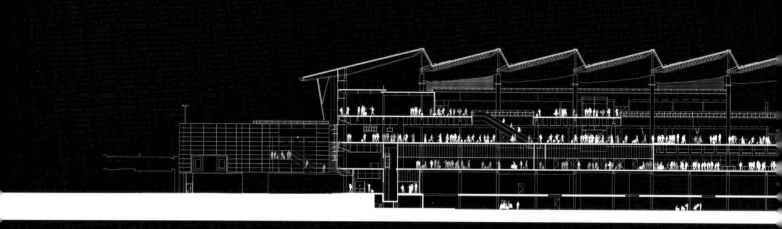
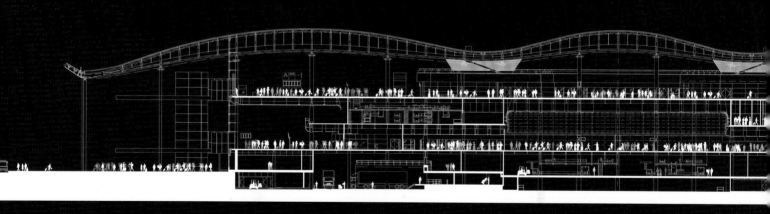

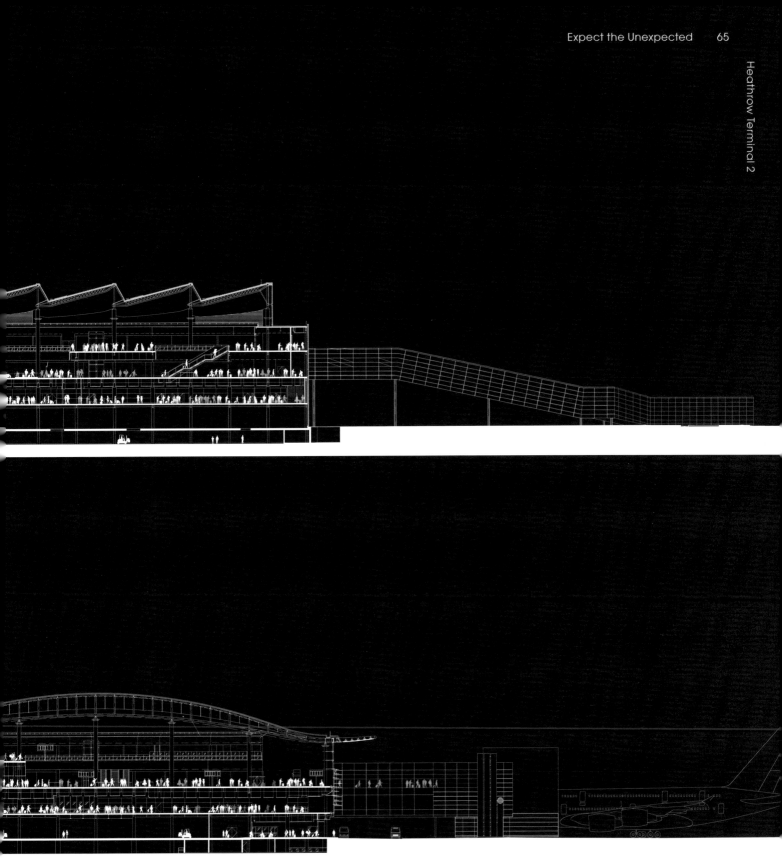

Client: IB Salut, Servicio Balear de Salud
Area: 67,000 m² (721,182 ft²)
Budget: €75 million
Status: Built

Ibiza, Spain

Can Misses Hospital

2008-2014

Can Misses Hospital is the only public hospital managed by the Balearic Health Service on Ibiza and Formentera. The hospital service serves more than 500,000 people in the region. The commission from the health service was to refurbish and extend an existing public facility into a new healthcare complex, tripling the medical area and taking advantage of the change to transform the way the staff works, creating a highly efficient entity. The construction and funding of this project was organized through a hybrid concession scheme in which health services have public management and non-health services are privately controlled. During the construction, a follow-up phase of consultation and technical control of the concessionary was carried out to ensure the quality of the hospital. The existing structure remained fully operational for the entire duration of the project, an important point because of the crucial role of Can Misses.

The design was conceived to recall the local architecture of Ibiza by using a fragmented construction that introduced white as the predominant shade. The Can Misses Hospital is thus well integrated into its surroundings, despite being the largest building on the island. Stripes of photoluminescent paint were added to the façades to make it glow slightly after dark. The building extension doubled the existing surface area, housing all healthcare services. The existing building was refurbished to house supplies and logistics facilities, freeing up a large area for future expansion or other uses.

"Beyond covering a social need, architecture must aim to elevate users' well-being in any given space."

—Luis Vidal

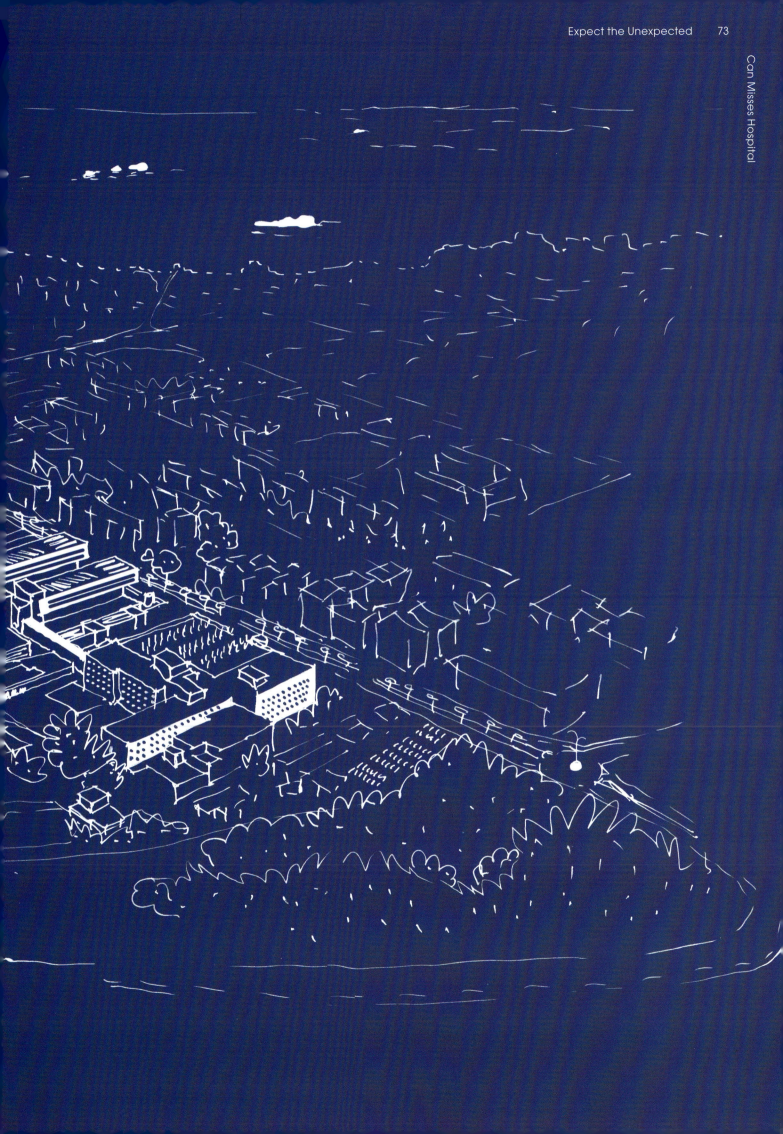

Expect the Unexpected 75

Can Misses Hospital

The color strategy for the façade was the result of an internal design competition that focused on the fleeting perception of the façade as the building is approached and passed-by in motion. This changing effect is enhanced by photoluminescent paint on perforated folded metal panels. This later evolved into the prismatic effect on the Àlvaro Cunqueiro Hospital metal façade as an innovative strategy to blend a large-scale building into nature.

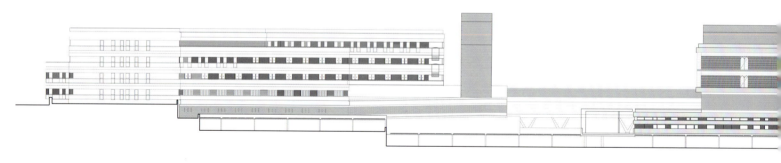
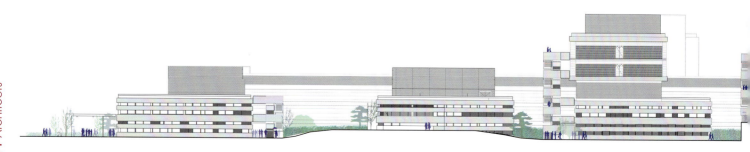

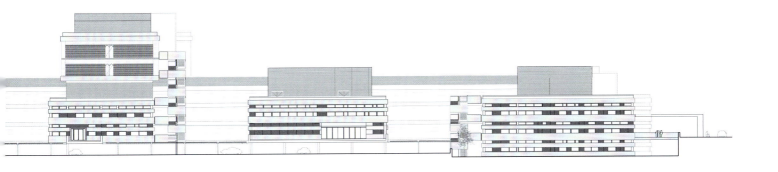
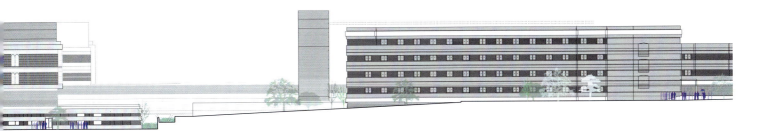

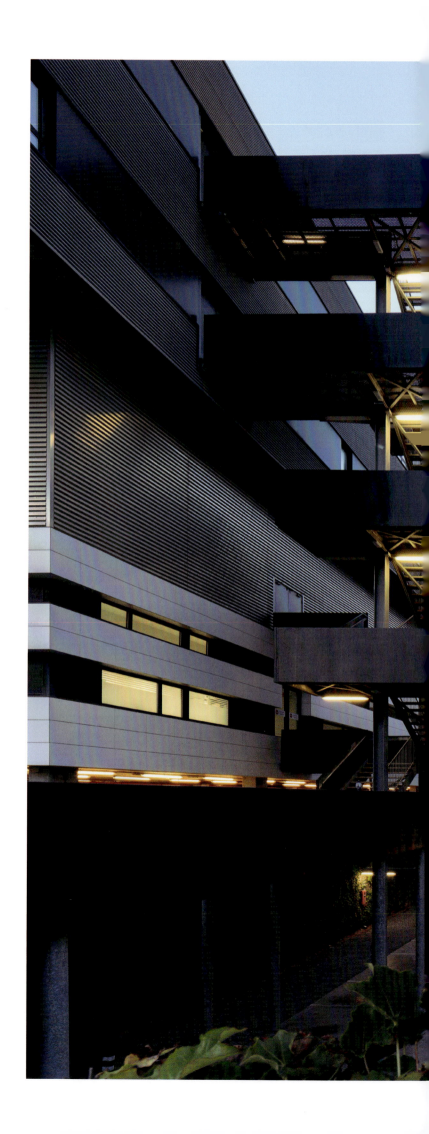

The hospital complex is articulated along a multi-level spine that connects the existing building and the extension, and maintains a strong visual connection with the old city of Ibiza.

Expect the Unexpected 81

Expect the Unexpected 83

Client: JV Novo Hospital de Vigo
Architects: Luis Vidal + Architects, Vicente Fernández-Couto,
and Jacobo Rodríguez-Losada
Original design: Valode & Pistre, 2008
Area: (total) 300,000 m² (3,229,173 ft²) ((hospital) 190,000 m²
(2,045,143 ft²) + (parking) 110,000 m² (1,184,030 ft²))
Budget: €238 million
Status: Built
Certification: BREEAM Certification

Vigo, Spain

Álvaro Cunqueiro Hospital

2011–2015

This university hospital was designed to serve the 600,000 residents of the city and its region and is the main health facility of the province. It is described as a node of knowledge, innovation, and health. The architectural design solves the challenge of merging two existing elements of public infrastructure into a new public-private building. It is one of the largest hospitals in Europe and was conceived from the point of view of the well-being of the patients.

The architecture is based on sunlit spaces and the presence of a therapeutic garden as elements to diminish stress. The building is on a hillside just outside the city of Vigo and takes advantage of the slope to gain a privileged position, which is integrated into the landscape. A clear division of the hospital's program was created. In the lower area, there is a stone base hosting the outpatient area. The large garden and public space above provide the main access points to the hospital. The six hospitalization blocks appear to float over this base, allowing for excellent views of both the valley and the garden for the inpatients. The inpatient area for diagnosis and treatment is in the highest area, with specialized and emergency access. A large glass volume hosts both vertical and horizontal communication and serves to connect the different parts of the complex, for staff, patients, and visitors. This connection also serves as a conduit for supply of the hospital.

The acquisition and assembly of equipment for the implementation and operation of health services in the new hospital of Vigo was co-financed by the European Union, under the ERDF Operational Program, Galicia 2014–2020. Early in its realization, the hospital won the award for Future Health Project at the Design & Health International Academy Awards. The hospital building has over a thousand beds, 150 consulting rooms, sixty-two diagnostic imaging rooms, and twenty-four operating rooms.

Energy efficiency was an important factor in the design, and the project obtained BREEAM certification due to the overall energy scheme. Strategies for passive design were used in conjunction with a photovoltaic plant, a thermal plant using biomass boilers, and LED lighting with automated control systems. Free cooling, using naturally cool air or water, is employed together with air conditioning and chillers that rely on energy recovery. Like Can Misses, Álvaro Cunqueiro Hospital was developed based on a Public-Private Partnership (PPP). Luis Vidal created a special prismatic paint for this project, which was later manufactured by Monopol.

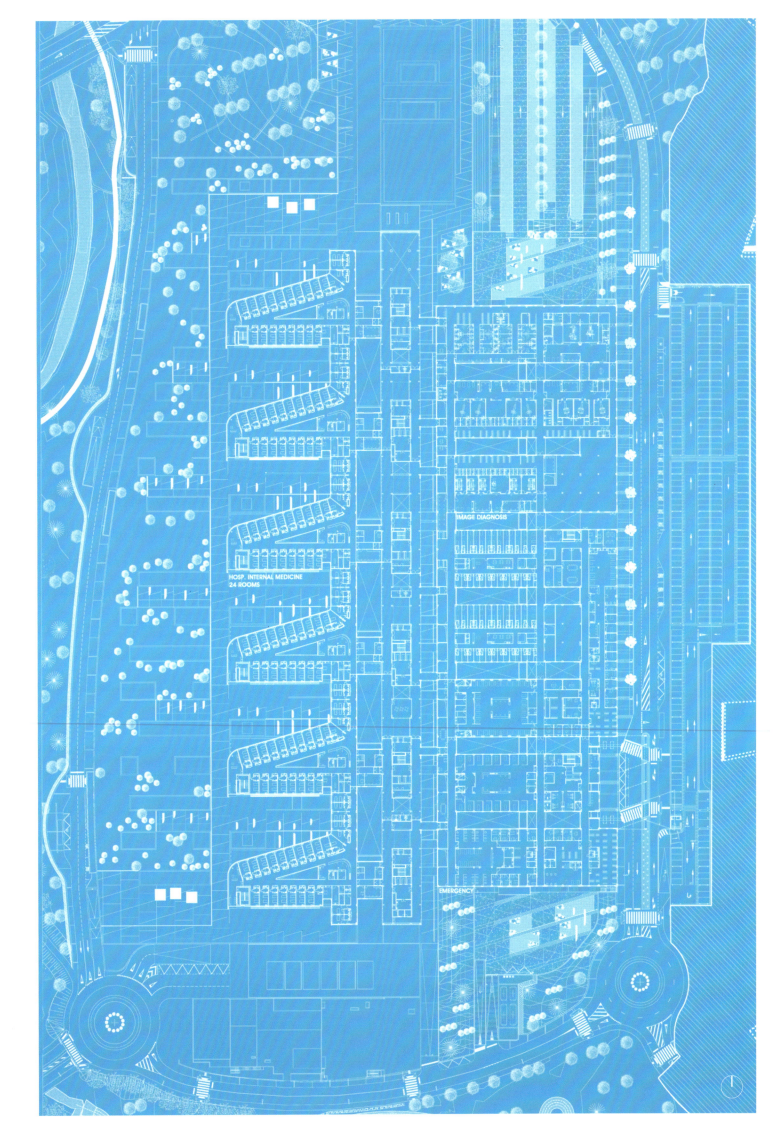

Expect the Unexpected 93

Álvaro Cunqueiro Hospital

The outdoor area has therapeutic gardens and timber decking and benches for gathering inpatients and visitors to spend time outdoors. It is perforated with sunken courtyards that bring light to the lower levels.

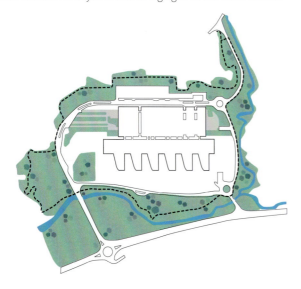

Senda biosaludable (biohealth path) is a 2-kilometer-long (1.24-mile-long) path along the Barxa River, which surrounds the hospital complex. It was a joint initiative between Asociación de Veciños de Beade (The Neighborhood Association — Social, Cultural and Recreational Center) and Área Sanitaria de Vigo (Health Area of Vigo) to promote sports and well-being. This path is filled with locals, especially at the start and the end of the day. During construction, the pedestrian paths were preserved and ecologically restored with vernacular plants, creating a green area for public use.

The prismatic paint effect, which varies from green to blue to white, helps integrate the large-scale buildings into their surroundings.

100　Álvaro Cunqueiro Hospital

"When you receive the commission to design a building whose scale transcends the urban profile that the city has generated for decades, you accept a double responsibility: to respect the past and to bequeath to the future. The main difference between the former and the latter is space and time. We must be more effective, more concise, and we must not forget that what made that feat possible was the determination and will of many."

—Luis Vidal

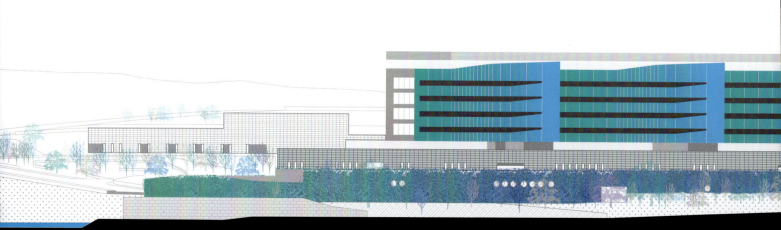

Expect the Unexpected 103

Álvaro Cunqueiro Hospital

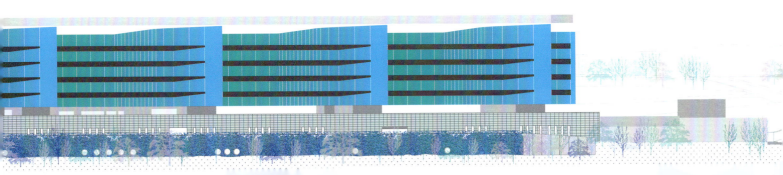

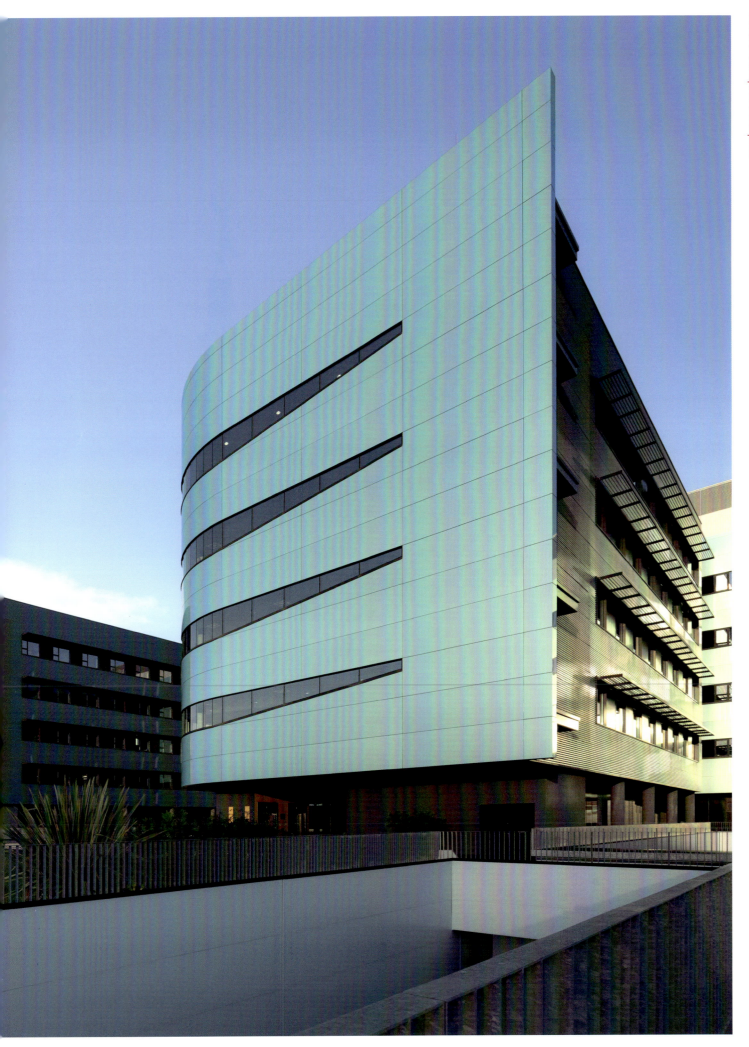

106 Álvaro Cunqueiro Hospital

Client: Fundación Botín
Architects: Luis Vidal + Architects in co-authorship
with Renzo Piano Building Workshop (RPBW)
Area: 10,000 m² (107,639 ft²)
Budget: €80 million
Status: Built

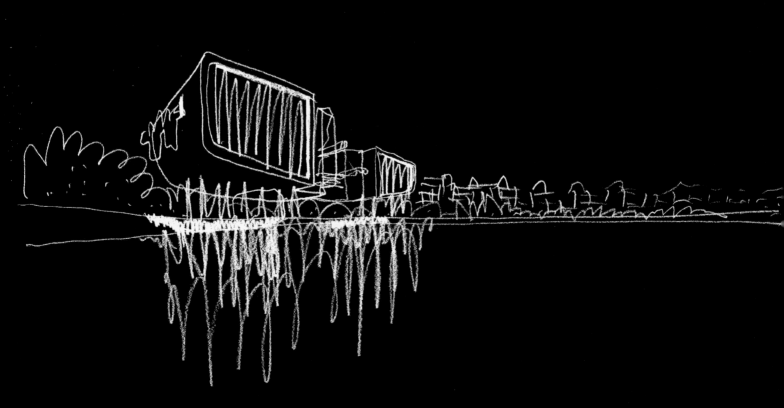

Santander, Spain

Botín Center

2011–2017

The Botín Center was financed by the Fundación Botín, one of the most important private foundations in Spain, established in 1964, with the aim of fostering the social, economic, and cultural development of Cantabria. The project was supported by the executive chairman of Banco Santander, Emilio Botín (1934–2014). The building is literally located on the Bay of Santander in the north of Spain, adjacent to the historic Jardines de Pereda. Half of its volume is supported on pilotis above the water. This device was chosen in order to not block views of the sea. Pearl-colored ceramic tiles intended to reflect the sunlight falling on the sea were used for the external cladding. The part of the building that faces east has a double-height auditorium that is cantilevered over the water. The second volume to the west, facing both the park and the ocean, has two levels of exhibition space offering natural top lighting on the upper floor. At 22 meters (72 feet) high, the center offers 2,400 square meters (25,833 square feet) of gallery space.

As described by Luis Vidal + Architects, "The quality of a design is also a result of elements that are not strictly architectural. In this case, the Botín Center is the result of the successful collaboration between two architects, Renzo Piano and Luis Vidal, with a common language: light, flexibility, transparency, and dialog with the city. All these elements generated a synergy in a design that has transformed the city of Santander. It brought the historic center and its centenary gardens closer to the bay, where the Botín Center is located. The building hangs over the land, suspended over the sea. It is composed of two volumes that host an art center, an informative programmatic space, and an auditorium. It was conceived as a multifunctional box, capable of hosting concerts, conferences, and creative events such as workshops. A series of light steel-and-glass walkways separate the two rounded volumes of the building, creating a new public square located above sea level. The Botín Center manages to intensely capture the sunlight, the brightness of the water, and the unique atmosphere of Cantabria. It is an architectural symphony at the edge of the Atlantic Ocean."

Expect the Unexpected 117

Botín Center

"The world is full of interesting sites and full of interesting people working hard at being their best. One must go out and learn from it all. It can only make us grow."

—Luis Vidal

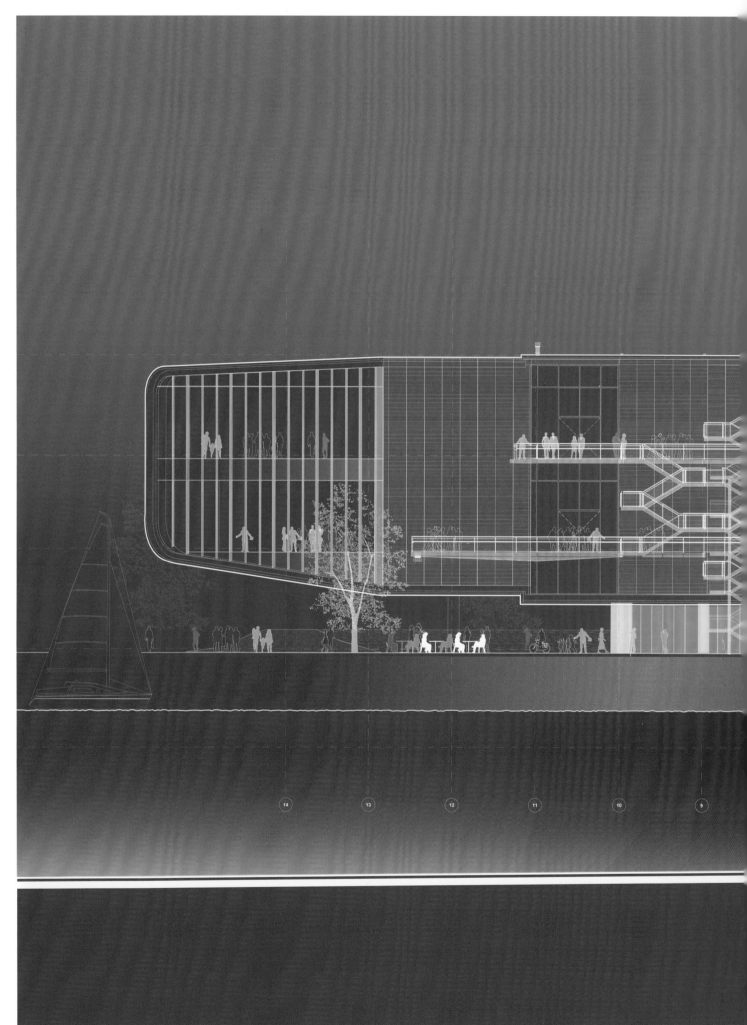

Expect the Unexpected 121

Botín Center

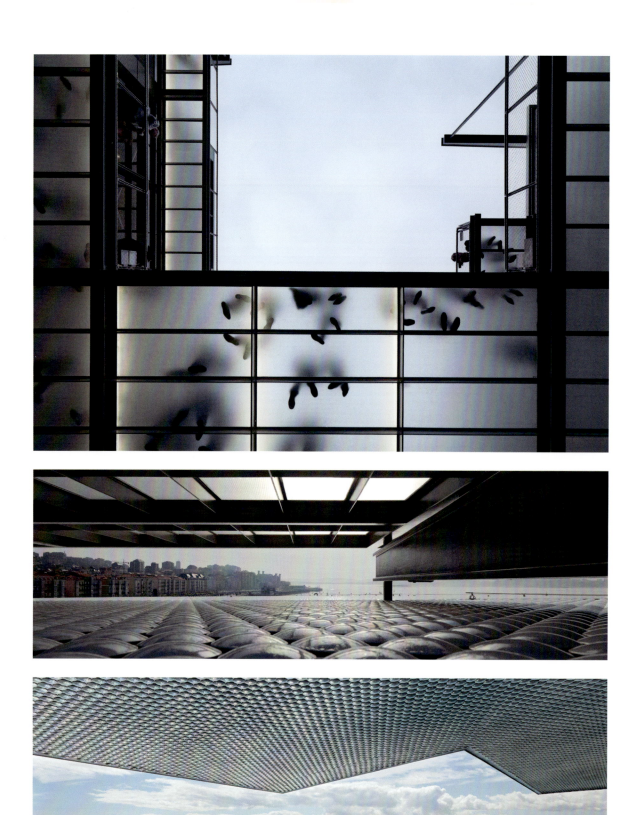

Client: Universidad Loyola
Area: 29,000 m² (312,153 ft²; Phase 1); 16,000 m² (172,222 ft²; Phase 2)
Budget: €29 million (Phase 1); €27 million (Phase 2)
Status: Built (Phases 1 + 2)
Certification: LEED Platinum

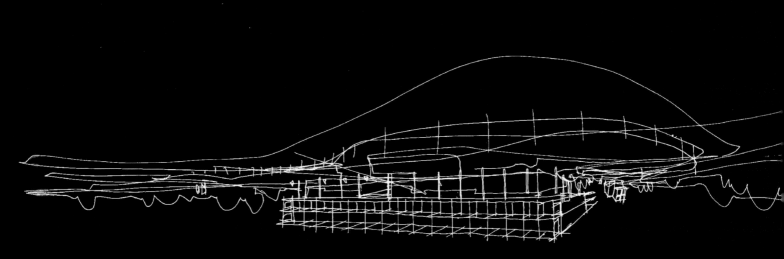

Seville, Spain

Loyola University Campus

In August 2020, Luis Vidal + Architects announced that its newly designed 29,000-square-meter (312,153-square-foot) Loyola University Campus, in Seville, was awarded the first LEED Platinum certification for a university campus. Loyola University thus became the world's first integrated campus to receive the highest environmental rating by the U.S. Green Building Council (USGBC).

The project took inspiration from elements of traditional Andalusian architecture, such as plazas and courtyards that were studied for breeze generation and self-shading. Controllable "sails," partly inspired from work the firm did on Heathrow Airport's T2 overhanging façades, shade these outdoor spaces in Seville's very warm climate.

Three key project objectives were the need for flexibility, the hope to instill a sense of community, and the integral strategy of sustainability. The north-south alignment was baptized the "axis of knowledge" and the east-west one is the "human axis," including a library and chapel. The intersection of the axes is clearly intended as a space for meeting and exchange. The alignments and modules, such as that of a classroom building, were intended from the outset to be repeatable if an expansion of the campus becomes necessary. Photovoltaic panels and a rainwater collection tank are part of the environmental strategy along with extensive passive design elements.

According to the architects, "When Loyola University commissioned Luis Vidal + Architects to design the first private university in Andalusia, the Latin root of the word universatis marked the starting point of a project that now has entered its second phase: universality, integration. To achieve this, one of the practice's characteristic architectural values was decisive: flexibility. Inaugurated before the Covid-19 epidemic, the complex boasts the flexibility and capacity for integration that make it an example of adaptation to health and safety requirements." In 2021, the client commissioned Luis Vidal + Architects to develop, design, and build Phase 2 in just eighteen months, a challenge that was met on time and on budget.

"Young generations have more information, are globally connected, and have acquired a commitment to the planet. We are in better hands."

—Luis Vidal

Expect the Unexpected 131

Loyola University Campus

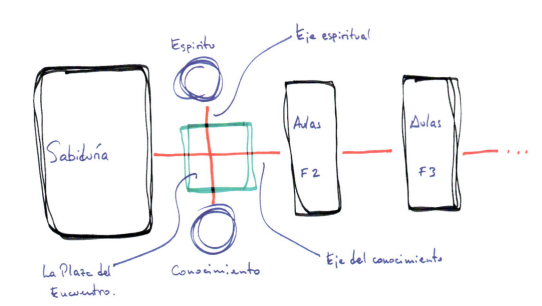

Conceptual sketch of the scheme arranged along two perpendicular axes: The north-south "knowledge axis" hosts administration, sports, and expandable education uses. The east-west "human axis" houses the library and the chapel. The intersection of the axes is a space for meeting and exchange.

138   Loyola University Campus

Expect the Unexpected 139

Loyola University Campus

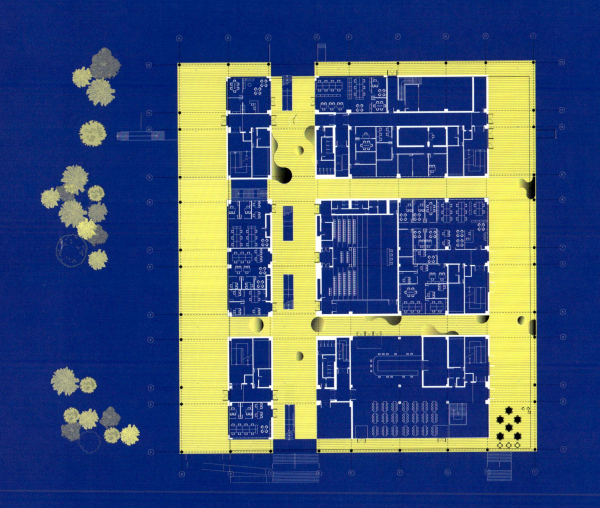

Phase 2 of the project included a Center of Simulation Education, a pioneering resource for simulation-based education in health science. The facility incorporates the full range of steps in a real-life clinic, from admissions to surgery, recovery, and discharge.

"Our greatest legacy to the following generations is the personal enrichment we can bring to them through our lifetime experiences."

—Luis Vidal

Expect the Unexpected 151

Loyola University Campus

Client: Gmp
Area: 25,500 m² (274,480 ft²)
Status: Built
Certification: LEED Platinum

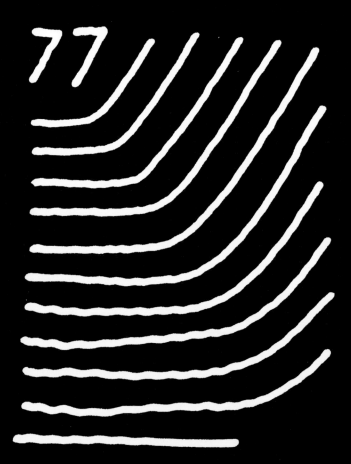

Madrid, Spain

Castellana 77

2015–2017

Luis Vidal + Architects was asked to transform the offices at Castellana 77, a 1977 building that had lost its identity and market value over a period of four decades. It is now considered a real estate highpoint in the financial center of Madrid. As the architects describe the project, the idea was to turn an invisible building into a visible one using the façade design. The result of the intervention of the architects is a flexible space, with a prominent identity that has made it the second most expensive office space per square meter in Azca, Madrid's premium district.

For this project, with light as the true protagonist, the practice used ETFE (Ethylene Tetrafluoroethylene) in an innovative way, creating a skin that allows the passage of light but not heat. They created a backlit wrapping made of thousands of slats with different curvatures that protect the building from the brightest sunlight, while maximizing user comfort and projecting a powerful image. The slats can be lit at night, which enhances the building's prominence in its surroundings. The goal was simply "to tame the light without being defeated by it." The firm calls it "a twenty-first-century Icarus designed to defeat the sun."

Parking for 170 cars was part of the scheme for this 62-meter-high (203-foot-high), eighteen-story building. With a LEED Platinum rating, Castellana 77 was the Five Star winner of the Best Office Architecture in Spain at the 2017 European Property Awards, and received a Special Mention at the 2019 German Design Awards.

The design strategy was to extract the building from its hidden position, making it more visible from Paseo de la Castellana (Castellana Avenue) and letting it shine with pride in its place.

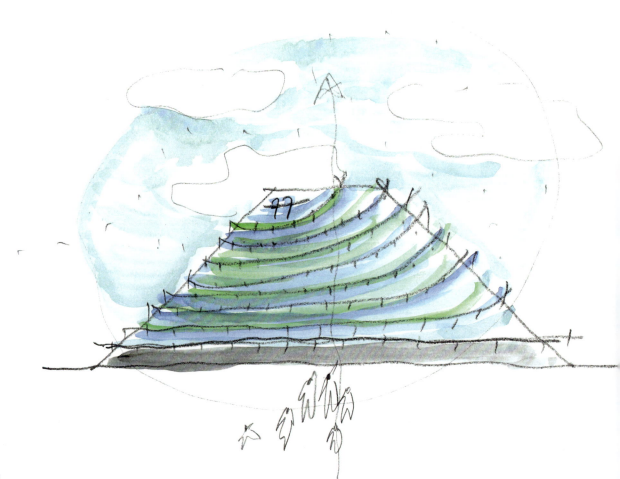

The façade was parametrically designed to provide efficient solar shading while also rebranding the building and bringing its presence to the main street. It is made of EFTE slats that can be individually programmed to be lit in an array of colors forming images and motion light displays.

Client: Dallas-Fort Worth International Airport
Architects: Joint venture between Luis Vidal + Architects, HKA, and Arup
Area: 14,000 m² (150,695 ft²)
Capacity: 65 million passengers/year
Budget: $200 million
Status: Built

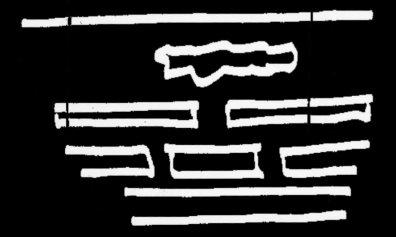

Dallas-Fort Worth International Airport Terminal D Expansion

Dallas-Fort Worth International Airport (DFW) is an essential infrastructure element in the United States and one of the largest transport nodes in the world. In 2022, DFW served more than 70 million passengers, while 15 million flew in and out of the original Terminal D. Delayed somewhat by the Covid-19 pandemic, the new terminal space opened in May 2021. The intervention on Terminal D of the Dallas-Fort Worth International Airport incorporates four new boarding gates, as well as 14,000 square meters (150,695 square feet) of concourse area to connect the original DFW terminal with the new one.

The new gates house modern waiting areas and lounges, a dedicated naturally lit and attractive international route with customs, and an extension to the baggage claim area. Luis Vidal + Architects have designed this space with large glass façades overlooking the airport runways, which provides a feeling of space and comfort. One of the key aspects of this technological design is the use of "View Smart Glass" that allows the façade to be used as a communication tool to show flight details and announcements. This dynamic glass automatically adjusts to solar incidence to optimize access to natural light and views, thus improving the health and well-being of the user. This will reduce energy consumption in the new terminal by 15 percent.

The design of the Terminal D expansion exceeds DFW's Green Building Standards (which are based on LEED V4.0) and performs 20 percent better than code standards.

When Terminal D originally opened in 2005, it had twenty-six gates. The new space was added at the south end of the existing building and will serve as a connection to the future Terminal F.

The expansion of Terminal D introduced improvements to security and technology, including electrochromic glass that allows natural light through the information panels on the façade.

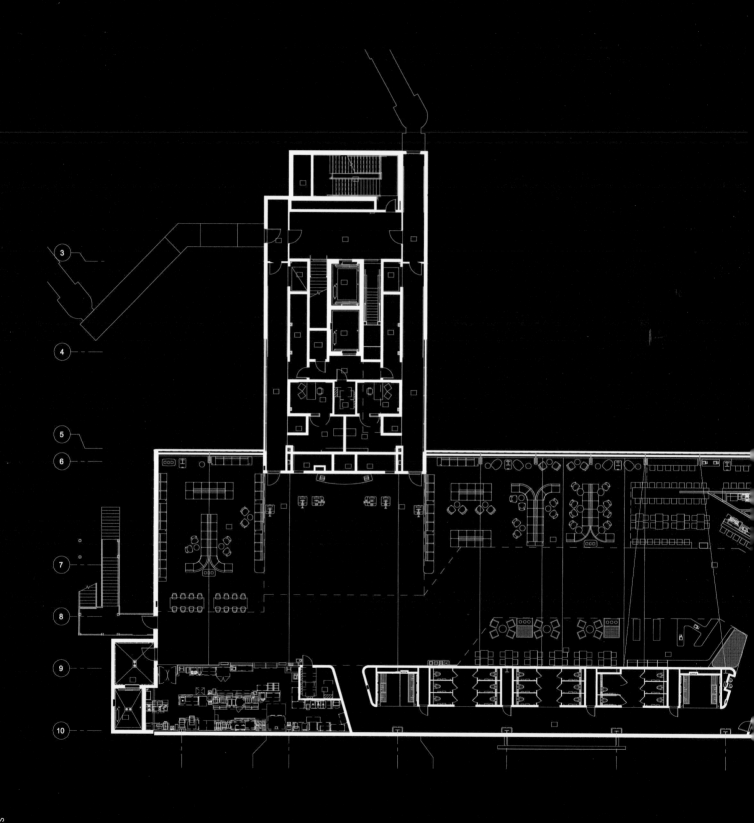

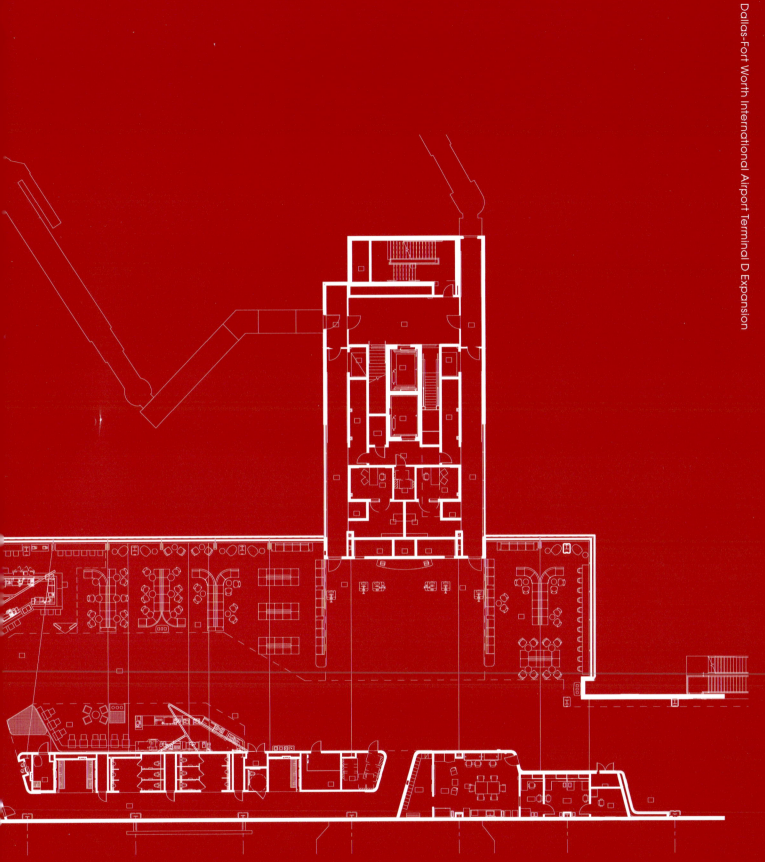

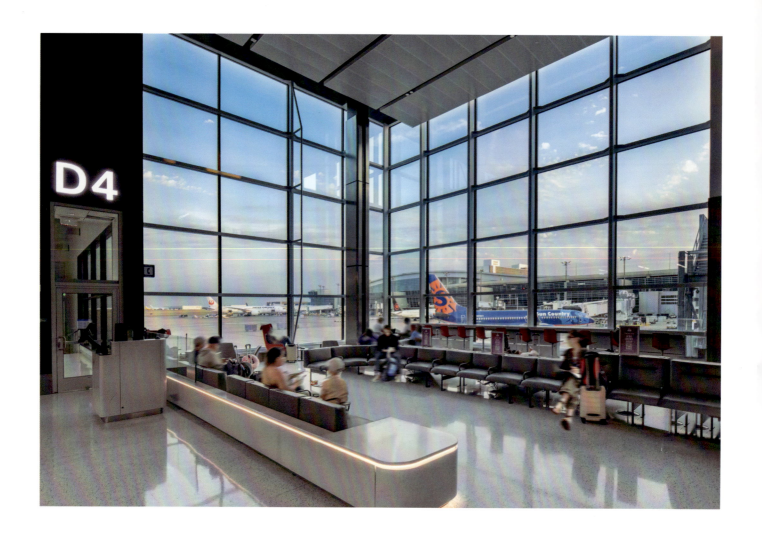

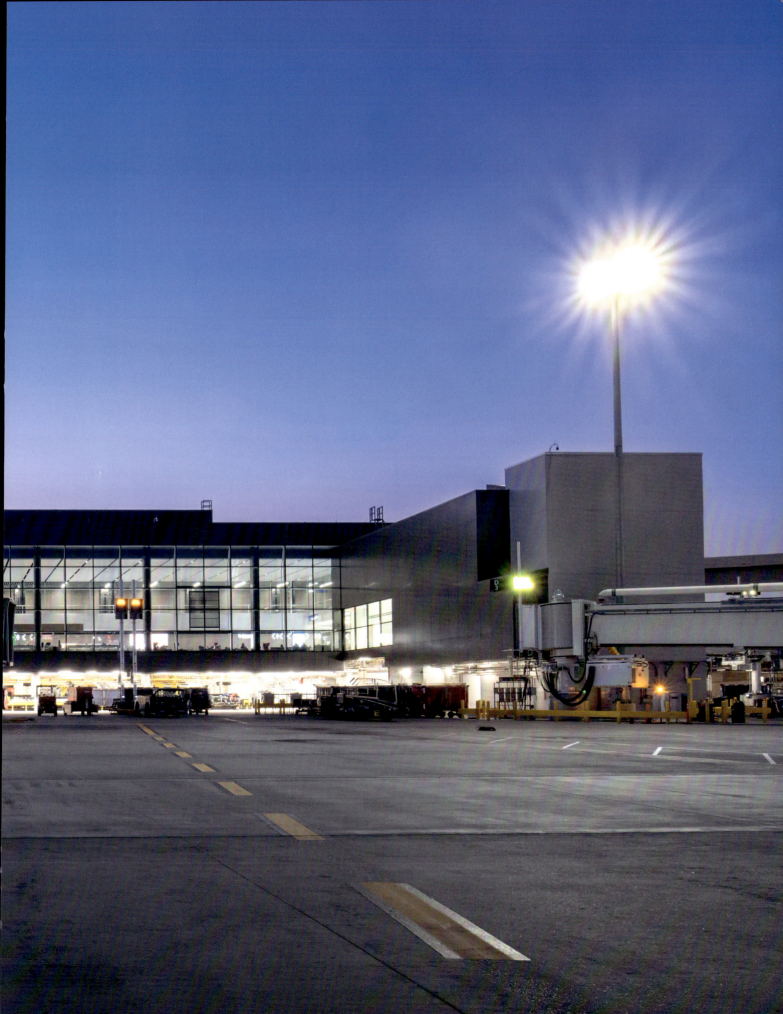

Client: Ilustre Municipalidad de Santiago
Area: 5,500 m² (59,201.5 ft²)
Budget: €8.6 million
Status: Built

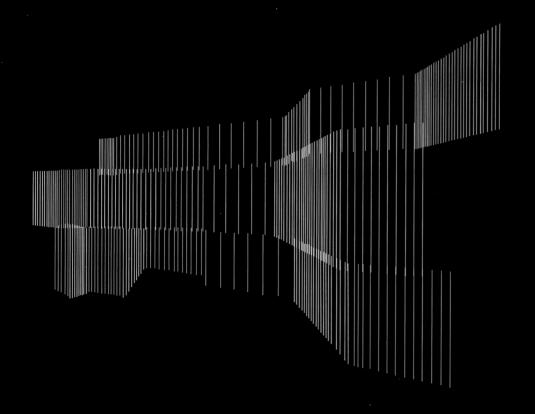

Santiago, Chile

Matta Sur Community Center & CESFAM

For architecture, the renovation of historic buildings inevitably involves a responsibility to preserve the memory and identity of a place. Luis Vidal + Architects completely refurbished a nineteenth-century building, the former Metropolitan Lyceum of Santiago, built in 1891, which is in the center of Santiago de Chile, and was restored to host social uses such as a nursery school, a gym, and an auditorium. The project also includes the design and construction of a new building within the existing plot for a CESFAM (Public Primary Healthcare Center).

The new structure aims to establish a dialog with the heritage building, combining tradition and modernity, using a homogeneous architectural language based on rhythm, materiality, and spatiality. The design of the new building is respectful and discreet, enhancing the original building. As a result of this interaction, a new public plaza emerges in the form of a connecting element between the two centers. The two buildings have a total built area of 5,500 square meters (59,201.5 square feet), which gives support to a community of more than 30,000 users.

The Matta Sur complex is a response to the challenge of cities, and to the need of today's societies for more public spaces, where residents and users can co-exist and be connected, fostering a sense of community. This project is also a step toward a strong and robust health system that can withstand epidemiological situations and crises, no matter how unforeseen they may be.

A "piece-by-piece" restoration and construction process was used for this project. The building site was divided in two and a team of highly skilled specialized artisans dismantled, restored, and numbered each piece of the original building, while another team worked on the new elements.

Expect the Unexpected 183

Originally a school, this is one of the few historical buildings still standing in a seismic zone in Santiago de Chile. The articulation in the existing timber structure enabled a full restoration of the original fabric. The new public plaza is a connecting element between the old and new building, providing a well-maintained and safe public space for the local community.

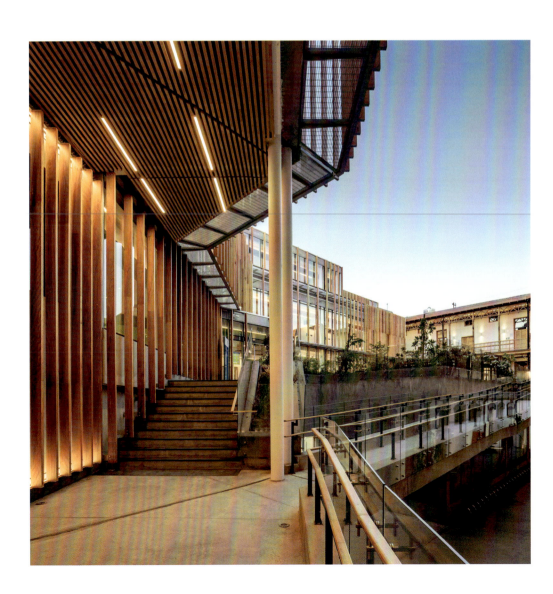

"Every idea is shared and collectively catapulted to an array of design options. I love to see the way the team emerges with innovative and creative solutions. We all get so much energy from it."

—Luis Vidal

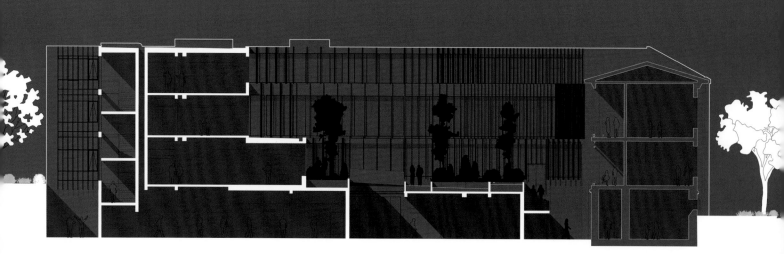

Client: SCL-CJV
Architects: Luis Vidal + Architects in association with ADPi
Area: (terminal) 250,000 m² (2,690,978 ft²) +
(parking) 100,000 m² (1,076,391 ft²)
Budget: $990 million
Capacity: 30 million passengers/year
Status: Built

Santiago, Chile

Arturo Merino Benítez
International Airport Terminal 2

2015-2022

The inauguration of Terminal 2 at Arturo Merino Benítez International Airport on February 28, 2022, now sees all international traffic routed through the new facility. The new terminal is expected to cater to approximately 30 million travelers per year, or up to 5,000 passengers per hour. All domestic flights now go through the pre-existing Terminal 1.

Terminal 2 is equipped with a modern control access and four piers, which act as a border between the landside and the airside. All its retail, food, and beverage areas are evenly distributed throughout, and the terminal's design greatly improves the visibility of the retail stores by directing the flow of travelers so that they pass in front of them. The retail space is now double at 18,000 square meters (193,750 square feet).

The VIP lounges of the airlines are strategically distributed along the halls so that the distance to the boarding gates is not excessive. Between the new control area and the current Terminal 1 building there are two covered parking lots with capacity for more than 3,000 vehicles. The roof of both parking lots is used as a large, raised welcome square, where the landscaping is the main protagonist. A variety of sources inspired a design specifically intended for Chile, where landscapes, geography, the flora and fauna of Chile, as well as the rich craftsmanship of its native people are highlighted. The landscape's "referential design" was a collaboration between Stantec and Amunátegui Barreau Arquitectos and the detail design and site supervision for Terminal 2 was by Luis Vidal + Architects, in association with ADPi. The work, which required a total investment of $990 million, was carried out by the French-Italian consortium Nuevo Pudahuel, which is made up of Groupe ADPi, VINCI Airports, and Astaldi Concessioni.

The new terminal complex can be further expanded to provide for 38 million passengers annually, as demand increases.

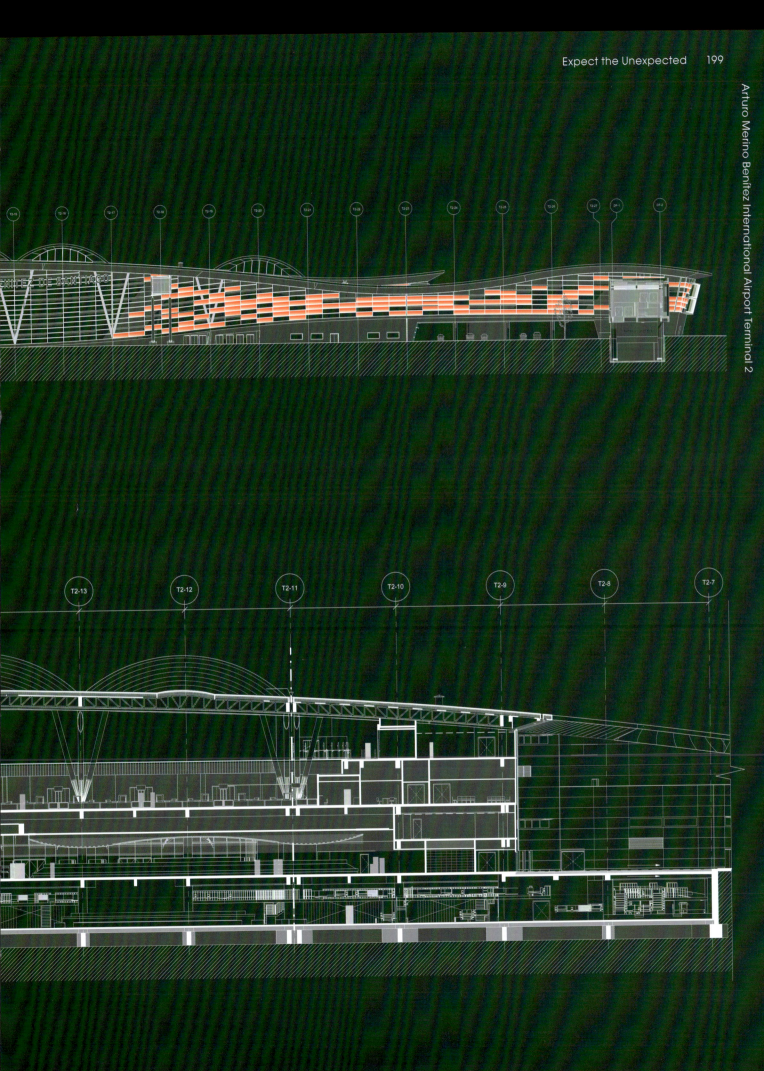

Expect the Unexpected 201

Arturo Merino Benítez International Airport Terminal 2

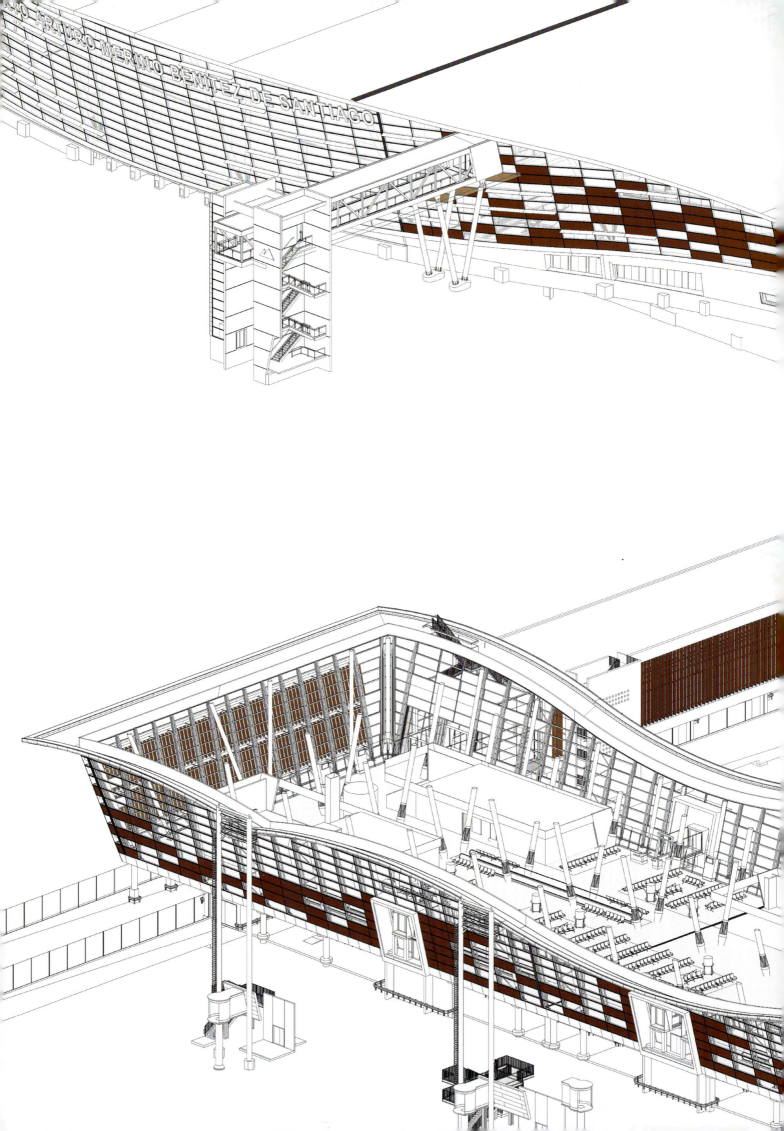

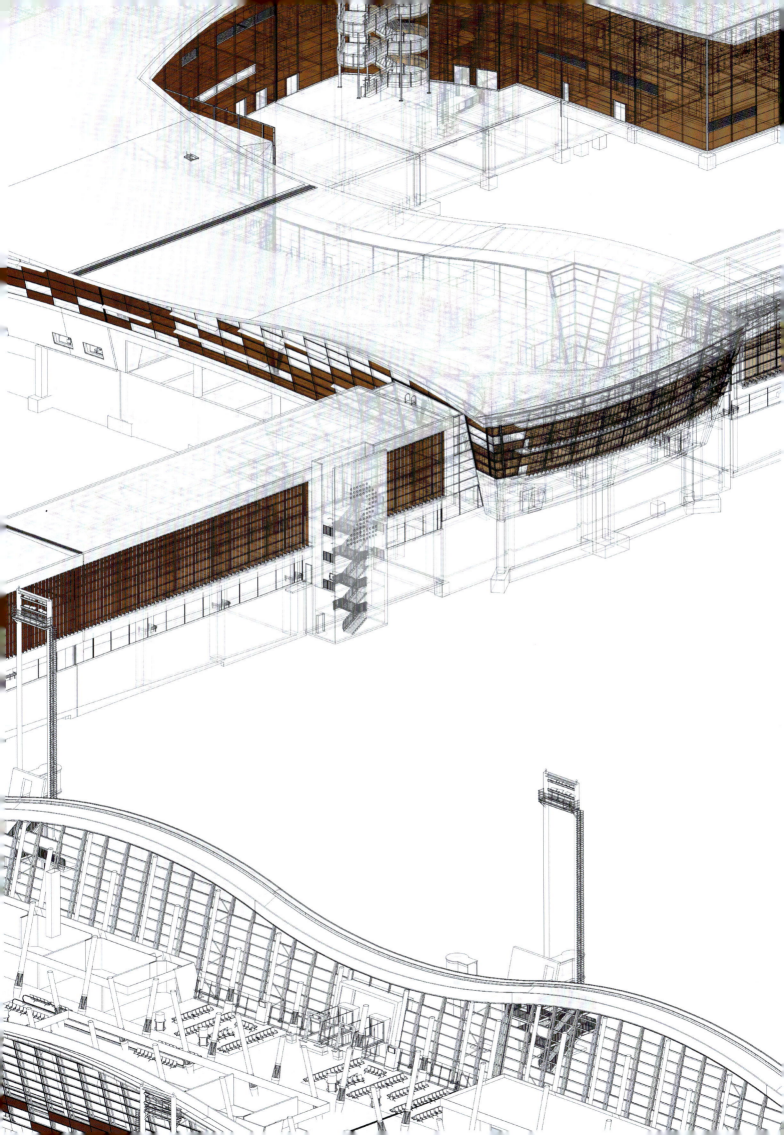

Client: Massachusetts Port Authority (Massport)
Architects: Luis Vidal + Architects in association with AECOM (AoR)
Consultants: (engineering) Thornton Tomasetti, Arora Engineers,
Dharam Consulting, Rider Levett Bucknall; (collaborative lighting)
Ricondo, BNP Associates, Code Red
Area: 30,000 m² (322,917 ft²)
Status: Built

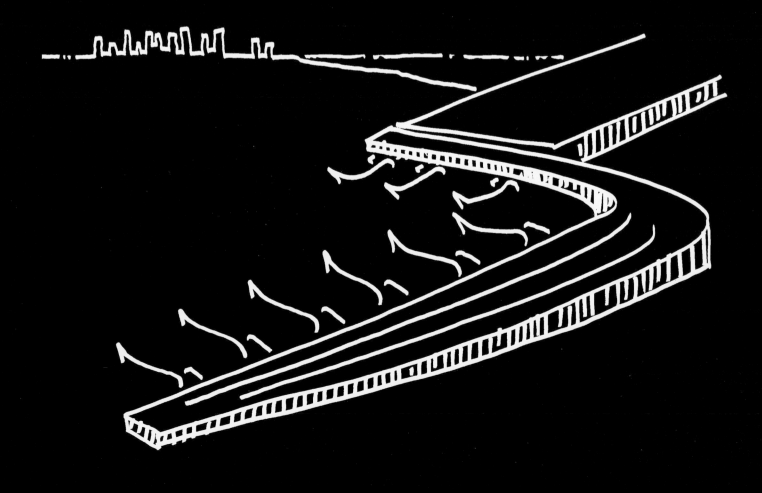

Boston, Massachusetts, United States

Boston Logan International Airport
Terminal E Modernization

2017–2023

Luis Vidal + Architects were chosen to modernize Terminal E of Boston's Logan International Airport in association with AECOM—one of the most ambitious projects undertaken by the Massachusetts Port Authority (Massport). It incorporates significant renovations to the international departures hall, as well as to the immigration and customs areas.

The roof and skylights were designed to maximize natural light and efficiency. The roof scheme makes use of two skylights facing north, composed of horizontal bands in the form of eyelashes that protect the interior of the building from direct sunlight. To the south, the deck gently touches the façade revealing a series of openings overlooking the Boston skyline. Intuitive orientation, spatial clarity, and a use of color are features that will transform the visitor experience in the new spaces.

Another feature that will make this airport unique is the exclusive "Boston Red" prismatic color on its roof, created by Luis Vidal in the Swiss laboratories of Monopol specifically for this project. It varies, according to the angle of the sun, from an intense shade of red to the orange and golden tones of the Boston sunset, and frames views of the Boston skyline.

The modernization of Terminal E is actually an expansion, with a new 30,000-square-meter (322,917-square-foot) building extending from the west end of the existing terminal and four new gates that will increase holding space. Phase 1 of the project opened to the public on October 12, 2023. Phase 2 of the project, also designed by Luis Vidal + Architects, will include another three gates.

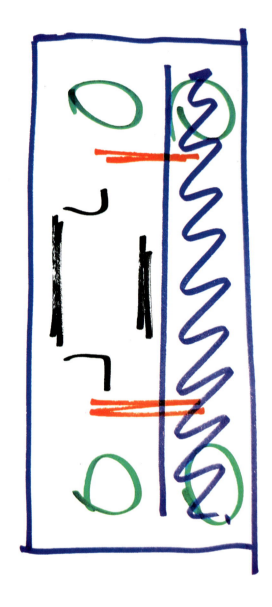

"Boston Red" is a prismatic paint exclusively designed for the terminal. Inspired by the colors of the sunrise and sunset over the water, the color changes from red to orange to gold.

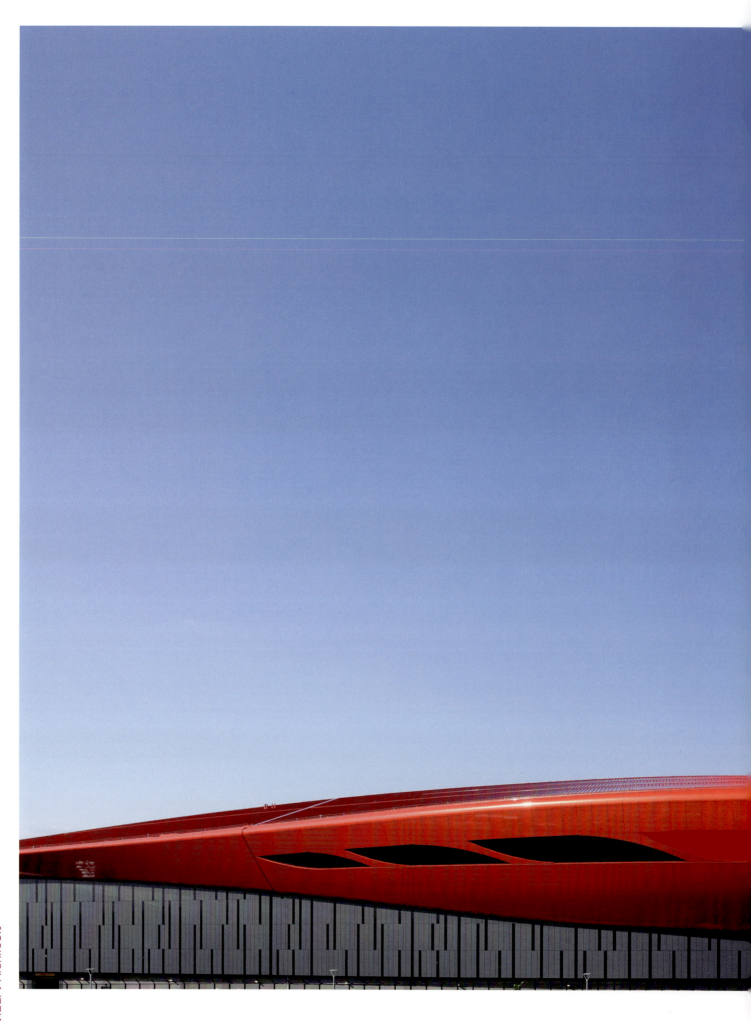

Expect the Unexpected 219

Boston Logan International Airport Terminal E Modernization

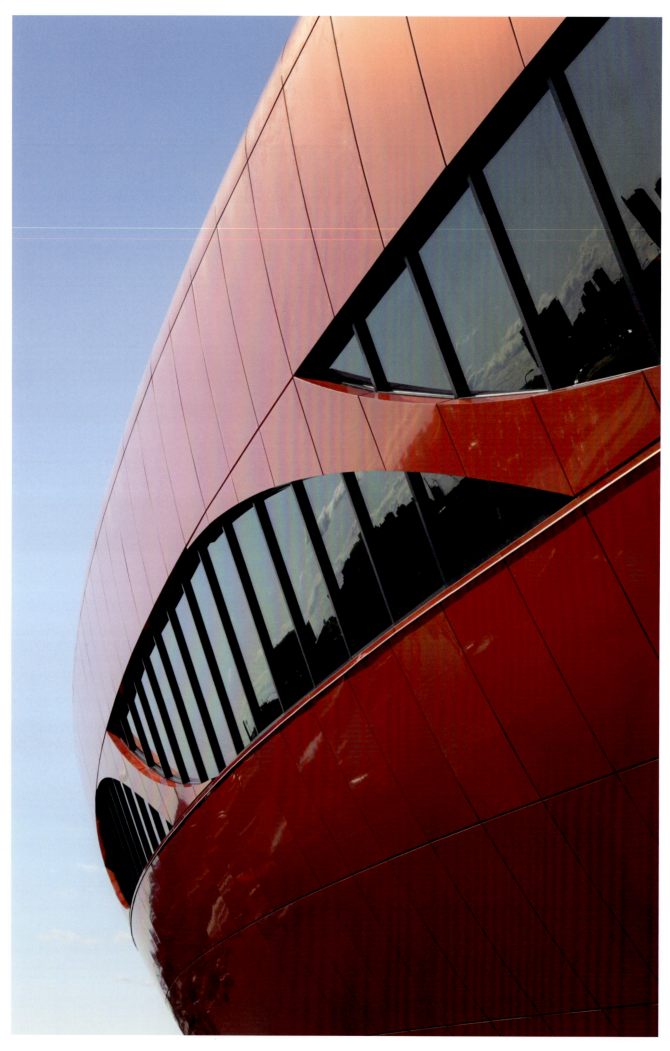

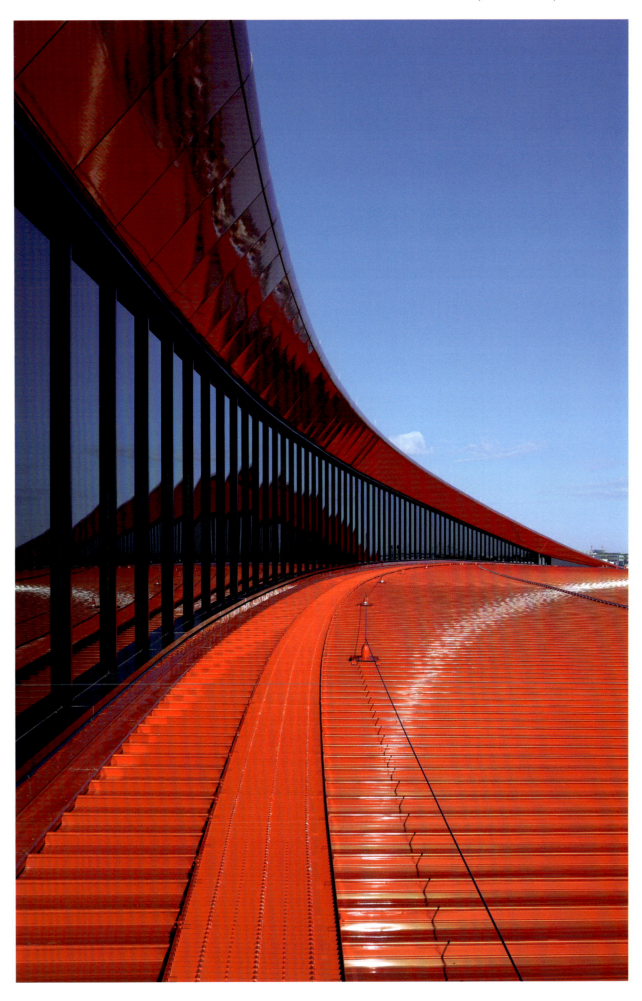

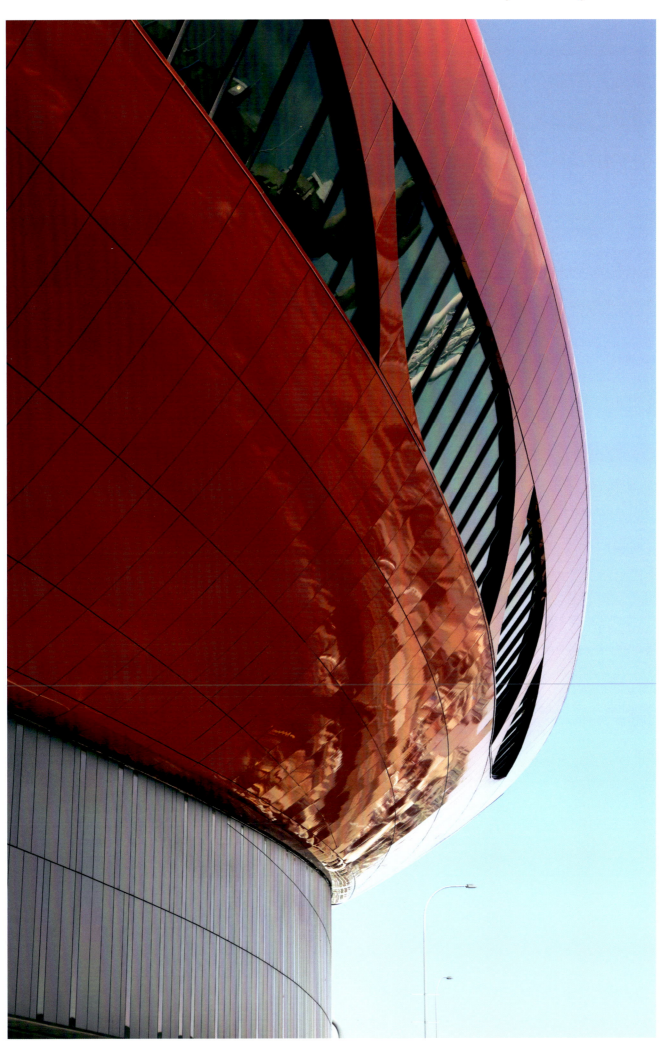

Client: Mutua Madrileña
Area: 20,300 m² (218,507 ft²)
Status: Under construction

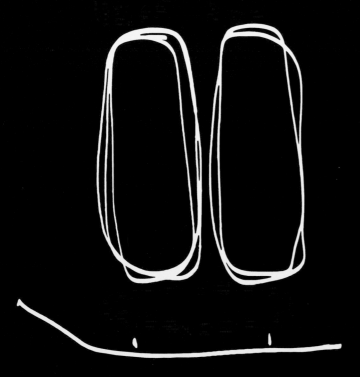

Madrid, Spain

New Colón Towers

2019–ongoing

The transformation of the New Colón Towers is based on three distinct ideas. The first idea is to extract all elevators from the core of each of the two buildings, and instead place them in a new adjacent tower. The area left empty by the elevator spaces is now occupied by new fire-escape stairs and rest rooms, freeing up the floor space that they previously occupied. The second idea is to join both towers that, together with the area freed up by the first step, provides a combined floor plan that generates approximately 850 square meters (9,150 square feet) more in footprint per floor rather than the original 300 square meters (3,230 square feet) per tower; also improving the net-to-gross floor ratio to 82 percent from the former 64 percent. The third idea is to relocate floor area from places where its value was minimal. Thus, the area of the former lobby (1st basement), the space of the former mezzanine above ground level, and the area of Level 5, together with the area saved by chamfering all eight corners of both towers, provide the volume and floor space that is built on top of the existing towers.

The structural system of this new volume is very distinct. The central core floors span as an overhang with no columns; the external skin is formed by curved glass allowing it to be self-supported without need for any structure.

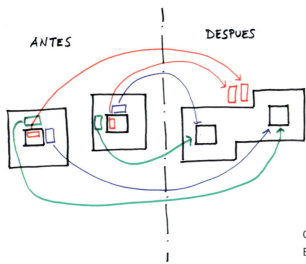

Conceptual sketch showing the reorganization of the space. Extracting the elevator from the core of each building and connecting the two existing towers creates one integrated building with more efficient use of space.

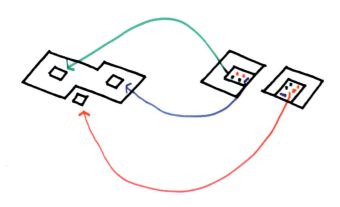

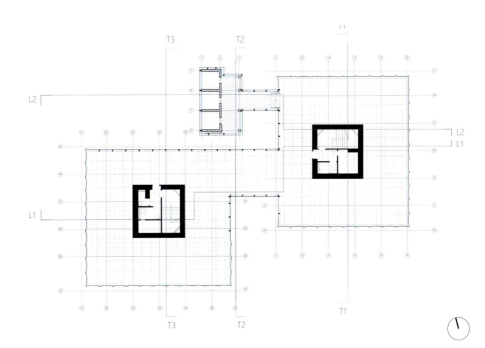

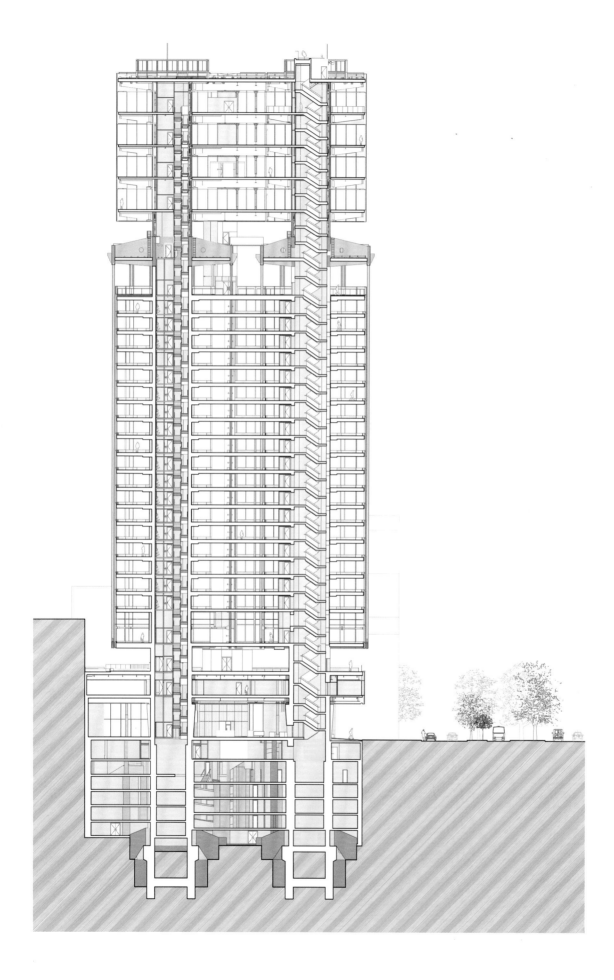

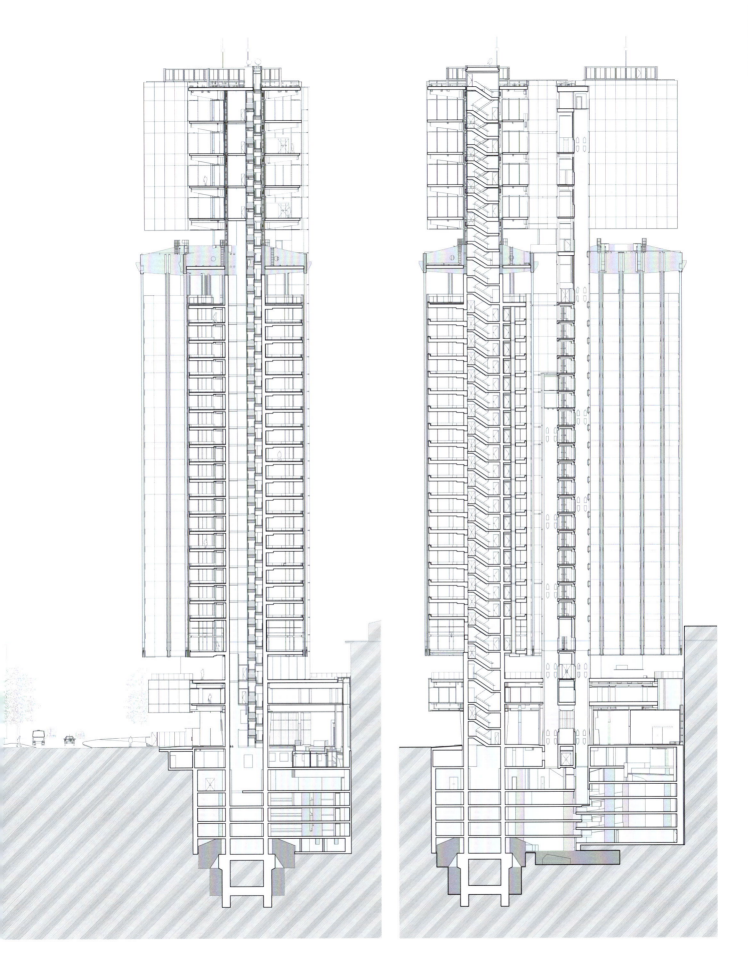

Client: Aena (Spanish Airport Authority)
Engineer: TYPSA
Area: (total) 340,000 m² (3,659,730 ft²); (expansion) 270,738 m² (2,914,200 ft²); (remodeling) 63,374 m² (682,152 ft²); (demolition) 5,888 m² (63,378 ft²)
Budget: €1.6 billion
Status: Design development completed

Madrid, Spain

Adolfo Suárez Madrid-Barajas Airport T4 & T4S Expansion and Modernization

T4 was designed by Richard Rogers Partnership (now RSHP/Rogers Stirk Harbour + Partners), with co-architects Estudio Lamela between 1997 and 1999 and built between 2000 and 2005. Luis Vidal was managing director and a partner of Estudio Lamela during that period. T4 is located 11 kilometers (6.8 miles) north of the older Barajas terminals, T1, T2, and T3. The iconic T4 terminal, with its undulating roof, had an original area of 470,000 square meters (5,059,038 square feet) with an added satellite (T4S) area of 315,000 square meters (3,390,632 square feet) already making it the largest terminal in Spain.

In 2021 Luis Vidal + Architects undertook a large project for the expansion and remodeling of the existing facilities of terminals T4 (and T4S), in a joint venture with the engineering group TYPSA. The project involves just over 270,000 square meters (2,906,256 square feet) of expansion and almost 70,000 square meters (753,474 square feet) of redesign, together with 1.2 million square meters (1,291,669 million square feet) of aircraft apron and taxiway areas. It is estimated that the airport will have to handle 60 million passengers per year by 2026, and this project is intended to facilitate that increase.

The land and air side areas of T4 can be enlarged independently, providing expanded areas for check-in and security. Thus, with an added 144 meters (472.5 feet) for T4 and 90 meters (295 feet) for T4S, it is possible to meet the increasing demand for check-in stands, as well as security and immigration controls. The T4 pier is being extended northward to accommodate new boarding gates for increased air traffic. Seven new single boarding bridges and three flexible ones (Multiple Aircraft Ramp Stand, or MARS) are located along the 360-meter (1,181-foot) length of the expanded pier. The T4S (satellite) expansion to a length of 414 meters (1,358 feet) includes thirteen new flexible boarding bridges.

The color strategy in T4 continues to be a highlight of the project, as it was for the original project. The use of color emphasizes spatial depth, aiming to offer passengers a unique experience of intuitive orientation. Yellow marks the central starting point, extending southward along a warm chromatic spectrum, while the north of the building is identified by colder tones. The expansion provides for phased planning that avoids interrupting the operation of the airport.

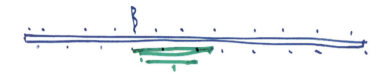

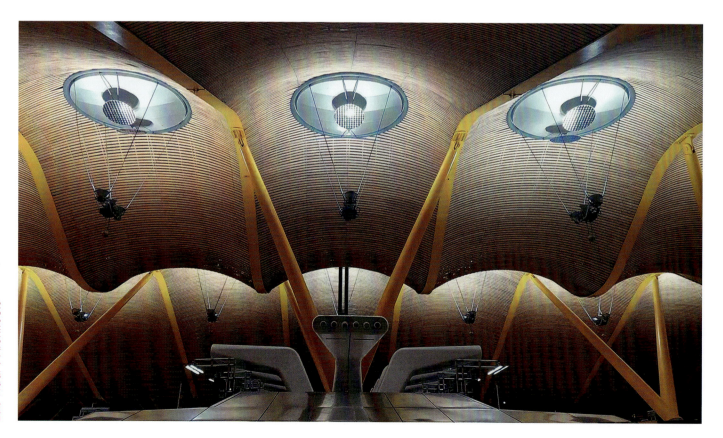

Adolfo Suárez Madrid-Barajas Airport T4 & T4S Expansion and Modernization

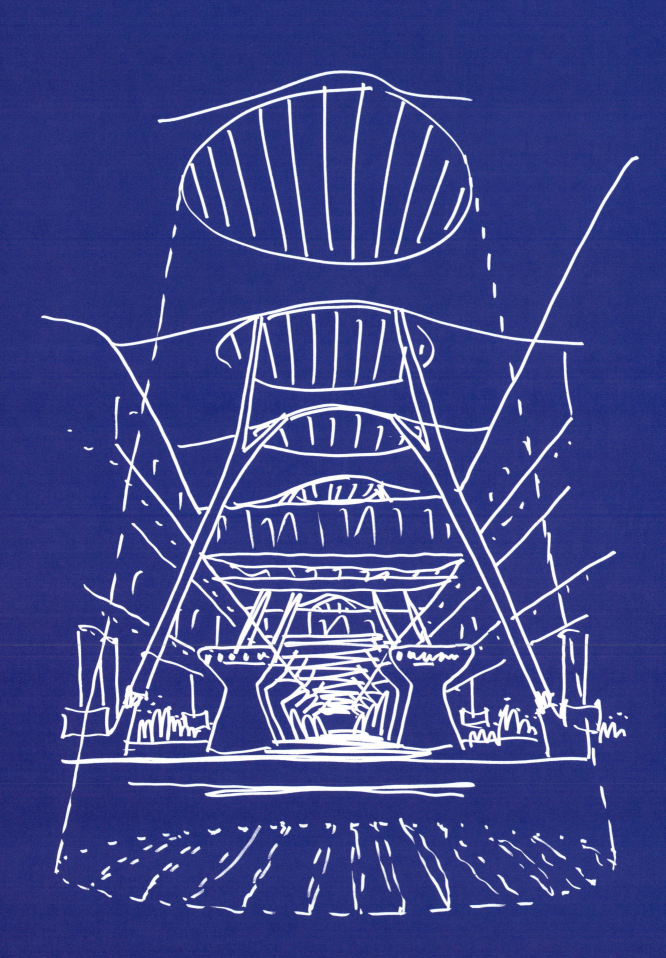

"Humans never cease to admire the beauty of what have become historical constructions. Architects must aim to create spaces that will remain appreciated for generations to come."

—Luis Vidal

Projects for the Future

Madrid, Spain

Loewe Excellence Center

2023–ongoing

Client: Loewe
Area: (total) 54,440 m² (585,987 ft²)
((built) 23,039 m² (248,000 ft²) +
(exteriors) 31,401 m² (338,000 ft²))
Status: Under construction
Certification: LEED Platinum,
WELL Platinum

The Loewe Excellence Center is a one-of-a-kind ecosystem that brings together talent and boosts knowledge while maintaining functionality for the luxury fashion brand. The architecture is inspired by the simplicity, fluidity, and constructive elegance of the vaulted ceiling.

The vaults are configured in a staggered, parallel pattern, and their scale is adapted to meet Loewe's technical requirements, and spatial and environmental needs for its production and storage spaces. Underneath the vaults, pairs of crossed arches support a perforated ceramic skin that allows natural light to filter inside. The overhang of the roof provides shade and protection and creates a sense of lightness to the whole building.

Pittsburgh, Pennsylvania, United States

Pittsburg International Airport Terminal Modernization

2018–ongoing

In the process of being updated to meet twenty-first-century needs, Pittsburgh International Airport will be able to process between 12 and 18 million passengers per year when it opens in 2025. The modernization will create an efficient and pleasant experience for passengers and users by consolidating land and air side operations into a single connected and adaptable facility.

The design combines nature, technology, and community, three pillars sustaining the city of Philadelphia and making it a unique destination. The region's rolling hills and vast woods are reflected in the sinuous curves and canopy of the roof. The warmth of the local community is embodied in the natural textures and tones of the materials, and the bronze terminal pillars capture the industrialization and technological advances of the city.

Client: Allegheny County Airport Authority
Architects: Luis Vidal + Architects in association with Gensler and HDR
Area: (total) 95,200 m² (1,025,000 ft²) ((new) 75,700 m² (815,000 ft²) + (renovation) 19,500 m² (210,000 ft²))
Budget: $1.4 billion
Status: Under construction

Santiago de los Caballeros, Dominican Republic

Santiago de los Caballeros International Airport New Terminal

2021–ongoing

Client: Cibao International Airport
Area: (total) 128,300 m² (1,381,010 ft²)
((built) 94,300 m² (1,015,036 ft²) +
(green area) 14,000 m² (150,694 ft²) +
(road) 20,000 m² (215,278 ft²))
Budget: $300 million
Status: Under construction

Santiago de los Caballeros International Airport, also known as Cibao International Airport, is undergoing a major expansion with the construction of a new terminal building, and the transformation of the existing building into a hybrid mixed-use space. The new terminal has two levels to separate the flow of departures and arrivals and will be equipped with the latest airport security technology. New roads and green areas will also be incorporated around the airport, and the expanded area will have a parking area connected to the terminal, and commercial, hospitality, and business services to complement the airport.

Celebrating the beauty of the region, the undulating roof and curved forms blend with the natural surroundings. The linearity within the interior is inspired by the harvest fields of bananas, tobacco, and coffee, and the timber roof structure and ceilings emulate the shade from vegetation. By evoking the region's landscapes in the design of the terminal, it creates continuity between the interior and exterior that draws nature indoors.

Selected Awards and Achievements for Featured Projects

Boston Logan International Airport Terminal E

   Massachusetts Economic Catalyst Award—MassEcon's 20th Annual Team Massachusetts Economic Impact Awards

Matta Sur Community Center

   Winner of Public Architecture Refurbishment—DNA Paris Design Awards

Arturo Merino Benítez International Airport Terminal 2

   World's Most Beautiful Airports—Prix Versailles

Matta Sur Community Center

   Finalist in New & Old—World Architecture Festival (WAF)

   Finalist in Mixed-Use—The Plan Award

   First Prize for Best Project Renovation/Restoration—Engineering News-Record Awards

   Honorable Mention in Public Buildings & Institutional—LOOP Design Awards

   Honorable Mention for International Architecture Award in Adaptive Reuse—The Chicago Athenaeum: Museum of Architecture and Design and The European Centre for Architecture Art Design and Urban Studies, and Metropolitan Arts Press, Ltd

Matta Sur Community Center

   First Prize for Public Building (Built)—Rethinking The Future Awards

   Best Mixed-Use Building or Equipment Project—Premio Aporte Urbano (PAU) Awards

   Winner of Mixed-Use Architecture Built—Global Future Design Awards

   First Prize for Best Intervention in a City and Historic Centers—Gubbio Awards, Latin America and the Carribean Chapter

   Merit Award for Adaptive Reuse and Historic Preservation—AIA New York State Design Awards

Loyola University Campus

   Best Innovative Project—Andalucía Inmobiliaria Awards

   Third Prize for Educational Built—Global Future Design Awards

Botín Center

   Award of Merit—International Association of Lighting Designers (IALD)

Castellana 77

   Special Mention for Excellent Communications Design in Architecture—German Design Awards

Arturo Merino Benítez International Airport Terminal 2

   Best Infrastructure Project—Construsoft BIM Awards

Castellana 77

   Finalist in Office – High Rise—Architizer A+Awards

Heathrow Terminal 2

   World's Best Airport Terminal—Skytrax World Airport Awards

Arturo Merino Benítez International Airport Terminal 2

   Winner of International Project: Building—BIM d'Or

Castellana 77

   Five Star Winner of Best Office Architecture Spain—European Property Awards

Heathrow Terminal 2

Green Good Design® Sustainability Award—The Chicago Athenaeum: Museum of Architecture and Design and The European Centre for Architecture Art Design and Urban Studies, and Metropolitan Arts Press, Ltd

Can Misses Hospital

Best Public Service Architecture—Five Star Gold Award—European Property Awards

Heathrow Terminal 2

International Architecture Award in Transportation—The Chicago Athenaeum: Museum of Architecture and Design, The European Centre for Architecture Art Design and Urban Studies, and Metropolitan Arts Press, Ltd

Best Airport in the World—Independent Travel Awards

Best Impact on Customer Experience—IWFM Impact Awards

Best Airport Award—Airports Council International (ACI Europe) Awards

Eco-Innovation Award—Airports Council International (ACI Europe)—Awards

Finalist in Public Building of the Year—LEAF (Leading European Architect Forum) Awards

Project of the Year—RICS (Royal Institute of Chartered Surveyors) Awards

Airport of the Year—Air Transport World Annual Awards

Client of the Year—The Lighting Design Awards

Daylight Project of the Year—The Lighting Design Awards

Public Building Project of the Year—The Lighting Design Awards

Best Airport Lounge—International Yacht & Aviation Awards

Nominee—Mies Van der Rohe

Heathrow Terminal 2

Five Star Winner of Best Public Service Architecture—International Property Awards

Five Star Winner of Best Public Service Architecture, London, UK—UK Property Awards

Finalist in Major Building Project of the Year—British Construction Industry (BCI) Awards

Winner of Industrial and Transport Lighting Project of the Year—Lux Awards

Commendation for Excellence in the Design and Installation of Shueco Systems—Schueco Excellence Awards for Design and Innovation

Finalist in Transportation —Airports—Architizer A+Awards

Heathrow Terminal 2

Champion of Champions—Green Apple Awards for Environmental Best Practice and Sustainable Development

Winner of Sustainability Building: Private Sector—Sustainability Leaders Awards

Winner of Health & Safety—National Constructing Excellence Awards

Gold Award—RoSPA (Royal Society for the Prevention of Accidents) Health and Safety Awards

Álvaro Cunqueiro Hospital

Winner of Future Health Project—Design & Health International Academy Awards

Palmas Altas Campus

First Prize for Best Sustainable Real Estate Project, Europe—Prime Property Awards

RIBA European Award—RIBA (Royal Institute of British Architects) Awards

Excellence in Design Award for Commercial—AIA (American Institute of Architects) UK Chapter Awards

Complete List of Works

Siemens-Vidal Personal Transporter
Madrid, Spain
2003–2004

Palma de Mallorca Convention Center
Palma de Mallorca, Spain
2004

Serrano Masterplan
Madrid, Spain
2004

Vallecas Social Housing
Madrid, Spain
2004

Reina Sofía Museum Restaurant Fit Out
Madrid, Spain
2004–2005

Granada Masterplan
Madrid, Spain
2004–2008

Expo 2008 Bridge Pavilion
Zaragoza, Spain
2005

Pamplona Airport New Terminal Building
Pamplona, Spain
2005

Private House I
Madrid, Spain
2005

Private House II
Madrid, Spain
2005

Tajo Hospital
Aranjuez, Spain
2005

Valladolid-Campo Grande High Speed Train Station
Valladolid, Spain
2005

Sustainable Façades
Palma de Mallorca, Spain
2005–2007

Infanta Leonor Hospital
Madrid, Spain
2005–2008

López-Ibor Neuropsychiatric Research Institute Extension
Madrid, Spain
2005–2008

Zaragoza Airport New Terminal Building
Zaragoza, Spain
2005–2008

Palmas Altas Campus
Seville, Spain
2005–2009

Valladolid Masterplan
Valladolid, Spain
2005–2010

Granada University Campus
Granada, Spain
2006

NH Alcalá Hotel Fit Out
Madrid, Spain
2006

RS chair
Madrid, Spain
2006

V76 table
Madrid, Spain
2006

Zara Via del Corso
Rome, Italy
2006

Port of Vigo Masterplan
Vigo, Spain
2006–2007

Madrid Justice Campus P-7
Madrid, Spain
2006–2008

Alcúdia Science Museum
Alcúdia, Spain
2007

Daroca Housing Complex
Madrid, Spain
2007

Heathrow Airport Sprint Eleven
London, United Kingdom
2007

Lanzarote Airport Terminal Expansion
Lanzarote, Spain
2007

Murcia Airport New Terminal Building
Murcia, Spain
2007

Pylon
United Kingdom
2007

Reus-Tarragona Airport New Terminal Building
Reus, Spain
2007

Sergi Arola Gastro Restaurant
Madrid, Spain
2007

Focus-Abengoa Campus
Seville, Spain
2007–2008

Private House Renovation
Madrid, Spain
2007 (Phase 1)
2009–2011 (Phase 2)

Zaragoza Airport VIP Lounge
Zaragoza, Spain
2007–2008

Palmas Altas Campus Fit Out
Seville, Spain
2007–2009

Castellana 66
Madrid, Spain
2008

Cosiensa Parking Meter
Madrid, Spain
2008

El Cañaveral Masterplan
Madrid, Spain
2008

Interior/exterior bench
Zaragoza, Spain
2008

Jerez Healthcare Center
Jerez de la Frontera, Spain
2008

Mesi-K table
Zaragoza, Spain
2008

Moinsa New Corporate Headquarters
Madrid, Spain
2008

Olympic Hockey Venue
Madrid, Spain
2008

Seville High Resolution Hospital
Seville, Spain
2008

Zardoya-Otis Industrial Center
Madrid, Spain
2008

Zig-Zag screen
Zaragoza, Spain
2008

Can Misses Hospital
Ibiza, Spain
2008–2014

Heathrow Airport Terminal 2
London, United Kingdom
2008–2014

Écija High Resolution Hospital
Écija, Spain
2009

Ontinyent New Hospital
Valencia, Spain
2009

Torremolinos High Resolution & Healthcare Center
Torremolinos, Spain
2009

Twist sofa
Madrid, Spain
2009

Valladolid Airport Terminal Expansion
Valladolid, Spain
2009

V-es door handle
Madrid, Spain
2009

Zaragoza Airport New Control Tower
Zaragoza, Spain
2009

El Palenque Business Center
Seville, Spain
2009–2011

La Marina Masterplan
Madrid, Spain
2009–2014

Garellano Masterplan
Bilbao, Spain
2010

Heathrow Airport Terminal 2 Car Park
London, United Kingdom
2010

Menorca Airport New Control Tower
Menorca, Spain
2010

Visigoth Section National Art Museum
Mérida, Spain
2010

Pontevedra New Hospital
Pontevedra, Spain
2010

Tlemcen Hospital
Algeria
2010

Toledo Visigoth Museum
Toledo, Spain
2010

Zardoya-Otis New Corporate Headquarters
Madrid, Spain
2010

Loyola University Campus Fit Out
Seville, Spain
2010–2012

MOOD sanitary line
Madrid, Spain
2010–2012

Bridge Over SE-30
Seville, Spain
2011

Clover table
Madrid, Spain
2011

Figurine lamp
Madrid, Spain
2011

Gerona Airport New Control Tower
Gerona, Spain
2011

Huelva High Speed Train Station
Huelva, Spain
2011

La Coruña Airport New Terminal Building
La Coruña, Spain
2011

La Coruña High Speed Train Station
La Coruña, Spain
2011

Portable lamp
Madrid, Spain
2011

Social Housing – Responsible Housing
Colombia and Peru
2011

The Size stand Construmat 2011
Barcelona, Spain
2011

Vertebrae lamp
Madrid, Spain
2011

Álvaro Cunqueiro Hospital
Vigo, Spain
2011–2015

Botín Center
Santander, Spain
2011–2017

Orense High Speed Train Station
Orense, Spain
2011

MOOD tapware line
Madrid, Spain
2012

M sofa
Madrid, Spain
2012

T sofa
Madrid, Spain
2012

Araba University Hospital
Vitoria, Spain
2012

VP Hotel Plaza de España
Madrid, Spain
2012

Castellana 43 Fit Out
Madrid, Spain
2012–2014

Navarra University Clinic
Navarra, Spain
2013

Quillota-Petorca Biprovincial Hospital
Quillota, Chile
2013–2014

Colorado Air and Space Port
Denver, Colorado, United States
2013–2018

Marga Marga Hospital
Villa Alemana, Chile
2013–2014 (Design development)
2018–ongoing

Loyola University Campus
Seville, Spain
2013–2019 (Phase 1)
2022–2023 (Phase 2)

Baltimore Airport New Control Tower
Baltimore, Maryland, United States
2014

From 2D to 4D
Tokyo, Japan
2014

Geriatric & Mental Health Services Magallanes Clinical Hospital
Punta Arenas, Chile
2014

Homat Building Lobby
Tokyo, Japan
2014

Huanchaca Ruins Cultural Park
Antofagasta, Chile
2014

Liceo Lautaro
Lautaro, Chile
2014

Magallanes Regional Library and Archive
Punta Arenas, Chile
2014

Mita Building Lobby
Tokyo, Japan
2014

Quinta Normal Park Greenhouse Restoration
Santiago, Chile
2014

San Sebastián de los Ángeles Chapel Restoration
Concepción, Chile
2014

Schwager Gym Restoration
Coronel, Chile
2014

Villa Alegre Municipal Museum Restoration
Villa Alegre, Chile
2014

Eloy Gonzalo 10
Madrid, Spain
2014–2015

Alameda-Providencia Masterplan
Santiago, Chile
2015

Jones Plaza
Houston, Texas, United States
2015

Mecca High Speed Train Station
Mecca, Saudi Arabia
2015

Schacht Palace
Santiago, Chile
2015

B&B Hotel Puerta del Sol
Madrid, Spain
2015–2016

Castellana 77
Madrid, Spain
2015–2017

C33 Executive Offices Renovation
Madrid, Spain
2015–2017

C33 Corporate Tower Modernization
Madrid, Spain
2015–2020

Dallas-Fort Worth International Airport Terminal D Expansion
Dallas-Fort Worth, Texas, United States
2015–2021

Matta Sur Community Center & CESFAM
Santiago, Chile
2015–2021

Arturo Merino Benítez International Airport Terminal 2
Santiago, Chile
2015–2022

Airbus Headquarters Campus Getafe
Madrid, Spain
2016

Ciudad Real Auditorium
Ciudad Real, Spain
2016

Ferroglobe Headquarters Fit Out
London, United Kingdom
2016

International Bank Office Madrid
Madrid, Spain
2016

Las Colinas Residences
Orihuela, Spain
2016

UC Christus Hospital
Santiago, Chile
2016

Denver International Airport Renovation
Denver, Colorado, United States
2016–2019

Macao Beach Masterplan
Punta Cana, Dominican Republic
2016–ongoing

Próceres Tower
Santo Domingo, Dominican Republic
2016–ongoing

Reserva Los Robles
Santo Domingo, Dominican Republic
2016–ongoing

Las Américas International Airport Central Atrium Renovation
Santo Domingo, Dominican Republic
2017

Las Américas International Airport Expansion and Modernization
Santo Domingo, Dominican Republic
2017

Latin Market
Washington D.C., United States
2017

Manuel Cortina 2
Madrid, Spain
2017

Velázquez 34
Madrid, Spain
2017

Boston Logan International Airport Terminal E Modernization
Boston, Massachusetts, United States
2017–2023

La Laguna Model Education & Work Campus
Talca, Chile
2017–ongoing

Julián Camarillo Business Park
Madrid, Spain
2017–ongoing

Madrid Nuevo Norte
Madrid, Spain
2017–ongoing

Samaná Destination Management and Urban Plan
Samaná Peninsula, Dominican Republic
2017–ongoing

Generali Building
Madrid, Spain
2018

Netclinic Medical Center
Santo Domingo, Dominican Republic
2018

La Fábrica Outlet
Santiago, Chile
2018–2019

Ezalia Office Lofts
Santo Domingo, Dominican Republic
2018–ongoing

Garellano Tower – Anboto Dorrea
Bilbao, Spain
2018–ongoing

Pittsburgh International Airport Terminal Modernization Program
Pittsburgh, Pennsylvania, United States
2018–ongoing

Pueblo Bávaro Church
Bávaro, Dominican Republic
2018–ongoing

Pueblo Bávaro Health & Educational Campus
Bávaro, Dominican Republic
2018–ongoing

Andrés Sabella International Airport Expansion and Modernization
Antofagasta, Chile
2019

Barcelona-El Prat International Airport New T1 Satellite Building
Barcelona, Spain
2019

Neom International Airport
Neom, Saudi Arabia
2019

Silvio Pettirossi International Airport New Terminal Building
Asunción, Paraguay
2019

Stansted International Airport New Terminal Building
London, United Kingdom
2019

Germina Foundation Care Homes
Madrid, Spain
2019–2021

Chagual Botanical Garden
Santiago, Chile
2019–ongoing

La Vigía Masterplan
Azúa, Dominican Republic
2019–ongoing

New Colón Towers
Madrid, Spain
2019–ongoing

Patio Embajada
Santo Domingo,
Dominican Republic
2019–ongoing

Arco Sureste Strategic Urban Plan
Santo Domingo,
Dominican Republic
2019–ongoing

Salas Piantini Campus
Santo Domingo,
Dominican Republic
2019–ongoing

Studio Legal Corporate Tower
Santo Domingo,
Dominican Republic
2019–ongoing

Adolfo Suárez Madrid-Barajas International Airport T4 & T4S Expansion and Modernization
Madrid, Spain
2020–23

FACCI New Pediatric Oncology Campus
Santo Domingo,
Dominican Republic
2020–ongoing

Villa in Ciudad Colonial
Santo Domingo,
Dominican Republic
2020–ongoing

Crotched Mountain Campus
New Hampshire, United States
2021

Eduardo León Jiménes Cultural Center Renovation
Santiago de los Caballeros,
Dominican Republic
2021

Quirónsalud Hospital Badajoz
Badajoz, Spain
2021

Solidarity Transport Hub
Poland
2021–2022

UAX Madrid Building A Modernization
Madrid, Spain
2021–2022

Arrecifes del Sol
Santo Domingo,
Dominican Republic
2021–ongoing

Cyril E. King International Airport Expansion
Saint Thomas, US Virgin Islands
2021–ongoing

Hemingway Village
Juan Dolio,
Dominican Republic
2021–ongoing

La Majagua Masterplan
Samaná Peninsula,
Dominican Republic
2021–ongoing

Maule Healthcare System Cauquenes Hospital
Cauquenes, Chile
2021–ongoing

Maule Healthcare System Constitución Hospital
Constitución, Chile
2021–ongoing

Maule Healthcare System Parral Hospital
Parral, Chile
2021–ongoing

New León Center Ciudad Colonial
Santo Domingo,
Dominican Republic
2021–ongoing

San Cristóbal Healthcare Complex
San Cristóbal,
Dominican Republic
2021–ongoing

San Pedro de Macorís Healthcare Complex
San Pedro de Macorís,
Dominican Republic
2021–ongoing

Santiago de los Caballeros New International Airport
Santiago de los Caballeros,
Dominican Republic
2021–ongoing

Santiago Healthcare Complex
Santiago de los Caballeros,
Dominican Republic
2021–ongoing

UAX Mare Nostrum University Campus
Malaga, Spain
2021–ongoing

Bluenest Vertiports
Madrid, Spain
2022

Fulton County Executive Airport New FBO Building
Atlanta, Georgia, United States
2022

Retama 3 Tower
Madrid, Spain
2022

Vilnius New Transport Hub
Vilnius, Lithuania
2022

Abha International Airport New Terminal
Abha, Saudi Arabia
2022–2023

Madrid-Chamartín-Clara Campoamor New Transport Hub
Madrid, Spain
2022–2023

CBS Headquarters
Santo Domingo,
Dominican Republic
2022–ongoing

Dye Fore 3 Villa
La Romana,
Dominican Republic
2022–ongoing

Los Pinos Villa
Santo Domingo,
Dominican Republic
2022–ongoing

Marriott Aloft Velero
Punta Cana,
Dominican Republic
2022–ongoing

Mirada Bay Ecotourism Villas
Samaná Peninsula,
Dominican Republic
2022–ongoing

Pittsburgh International Airport Airside Renovation
Pittsburgh, Pennsylvania,
United States
2022–ongoing

The Grand Tower by Contemega
Santo Domingo,
Dominican Republic
2022–ongoing

Velero Commercial
Punta Cana,
Dominican Republic
2022–ongoing

Velero Convention Center
Punta Cana,
Dominican Republic
2022–ongoing

Velero Offices
Punta Cana,
Dominican Republic
2022–ongoing

Salas Piantini Corporate Office Renovation
Santo Domingo,
Dominican Republic
2023

El Valle Samaná
Samaná Peninsula,
Dominican Republic
2023–ongoing

Loewe Excellence Center
Madrid, Spain
2023–ongoing

Pensacola International Airport Terminal Building Expansion
Pensacola, Florida, United States
2023–ongoing

Team

Alfredo Abarca   Gustavo Abelenda   Nawal Abou   Joao Abreu   Fernanda Adonis   José Aguado   Javier Aguirre   Ali Akbour   Carlos Alba   Raquel Albarrán   Jaime Alberdi   Antonio Albertos   Patricia Albesa   Carlos Albi   Luis Alfaro   Ismael Alfonso   Patricia Allona   Beatriz Almeida   Alejandra Alonso   Bárbara Alonso   Carlota Alonso   Osvaldo Alonso   Rocío Alonso   Rosa Alonso   Guillermo Álvarez   Ignacio Álvarez-Monteserín   María Álvarez-Santullano   Bianca Amerini   Constanza Andrade   Cristina Andreu   Carmen Andújar   Trinidad Antunovic   Balsam Aoun   Michelle Aoun   Sabina Aparicio   Mar Araujo   María José Araya   María Arce   Fernando Arenas   Ana Argüelles   Paz Armenta   Alberto Arostegui   Ariadna Arranz   Andoni Arrizabalaga   Constanza Astaburuaga   María Astiaso   Asier Aurrekoetxea   David Ávila   Nick Axel   Adriana Ball   Claudio Balluff   Beatriz Barco   Guillermo Barra   Álvar Barrera   Juan Carlos Barros   Javier Bartret   María Basílico   Margarita Bedmar   Fernando Bello   Laura Belmonte   Yamila Benítez   Virginia Bermell-Scorcia   Alessandro Biondi   Alfredo Biosca   Carmen Bisonó   Ana Blanche   Tatiana Blas   Alejandra Boquin   Adriana Borja   Giovani Bosmediano   José Braulio   Juan Bueno   Bernat Burguera   Berta Cabañas   Thiare Cabrera   Daniela Calderón   Fernando Callejón   Eduardo Calvo   Carlota Canaán   Patricia Cantero   Irene Capote   Laura Cappa   Isidora Cárdenas   Ismael Cárdenas   Marta Cariñena   Álvaro Carmona   Hugo Carrasco   Belén Carrillo   Lorena Carvalho   Gonzalo Casado   Jean Pierre Casillas   Alicia Castillo   María Castillo   Irene Castrillo   Fernando Celaya   Cristina Chaves   Valentina Chisci   Juan José Cid   Eva Clark   Esperanza Cobo   Alberto Coelho   Luis Colino   María Comella   José Ignacio Comparini   José Cortines   Eva Couto   Belén Crespi   Esther Crespo   Joe Cruz   Sebastián Cruz   María Cuadra   Marta Cumellas   Cristina D´Cotta   Zelia da Costa   Max Daiber   Sandra Davies   Chris Dawson   Begoña de Andrés   Icíar de Basterrechea   Alfredo de Blas   Itziar de Francisco   Antonio de la Carrera   Pedro de Lachiondo   Lucía de Molina   Félix de Moya   Ana Claudia de Queiroz   Alba del Castillo   Sara del Piñal   Marta Del Toro   Anyelina Delgado   Leidy Delgado   Javiera Díaz   Obie Díaz   Pablo Doblado   Javier Domínguez   Jorge Domínguez   Katherine Donoso   Daniela Duarte   Juan Esteban Duque   Louis Edwards   Oscar Ignacio Encabo   Franco Encina   Alfredo Entrala   Nuria Espina   Paula Espínola   Natalia Paz Espósito   Tania Estay   Karina Estévez   Beatriz Eyries   Juan Fajardo   Andrea Felip   Laura Fermoso   Constanza Fernández   Cristina Fernández   José Benito Fernández   Julián Fernández   Alejandra Fernández de Araoz   Pablo Fernández Villa Sánchez   David Fernández-Feito   Beatriz Fernández-Bermejo   David Fernández-Llompart   José Luis Fernández-Morais   Sonia Ferraras   Jorge Ferreiro   Álvaro Ferrer   Mayra Ferruz   Gonzalo Fidalgo   Susanne Forner   Ana Belén Franco   Anja Franco   Francisco Javier Franco   Lara Freire   Beatriz Freiria   María Fresneda   Ester Fuente   Patricio Fuentealba   José Gad   Hernán Gaete   Jesús Gallego   Jaime Galovart   Amparo Galván   Cristina Galván   Marta Gálvez   Carlos García   Emilio García   Esteban García   Evangelista García   Guillermo García   Jason García   Jorge García   Luis García   María Eugenia García   Marina García   Marta García   Pablo García   Victoria García   Magdalena García de Durango   Claudia García-Nieto   Nicolas Garín   Gonzalo Garrido   Isabel Gil   Paula Gil de Bernabé   Jaime Gimeno   Agustina Giudici   Nora Goch   Jesús Gómez   José Gómez   Laura Gómez   Raúl Gómez   Sassha Gómez   Nuria Gómez del Campillo   Alejandro González   Natalia González   Ricardo González   Rocío González   Sandra González   Victoria González-Aller

Carlos González-Gutiérrez   Carlos González-Mazo   Angie Graciano   Florian Graumann   Lucía Greco   Cristian Gutiérrez   Mónica Gutiérrez   Sonia Gutiérrez   Ana Gutiérrez de Tovar   Nima Haghighatpour   Jim Henry   Arturo Hernández   Laura Herreros   Eva Higueras   Trinidad Hildebrandt   Bill Hogan   Baylee Holder   Juan Huarte   José Miguel Ibáñez   Zainab Ibrahim   Ángel Inclán   Andrés Infantes   Joaquín Ivanovic   Silvia Izaguirre   Néstor Jara   Matilde Jaraiz   Camila Jiménez   Carlos Jiménez   Moira Johnson   Krists Karklins   Sanae Khalil   Andrew Kirchhoff   Marcin Koltunski   Pablo Labra   Itziar Lamy   Consuelo Larrea   Claudia Leal   Reyes León   Juan Francisco Letelier   José Luis Lleó   Beatriz Llorente   Carlos López   David López   Jugatx López   Lorena López   María López   Paula López   Arturo López-Bachiller   Julio Isidro Lozano   Patricia Lozano   Sebastián Lucero   Lola Magaz   Joaquín Maire   Carlos Maldonado   Maryuris Maldonado   Ana Marco   Sarai Marcos   Pablo Marín   Rafael Marmolejos   Macarena Márquez   Clara Martín   Paloma Martín   Rocío Martín   Silvia Martín   Álvaro Martínez   Brenda Martínez   Diana Martínez   Elisa Martínez   Francisco Martínez   Humberto Martínez   Nazzira Martínez   Nuria Martínez   Gabriel Mascaró   Guillermo Mascort   Javier Matamala   José Miguel Mättig   Jorge Maulme   Álvaro Mayoral   Camille Mccollum   Rafael Meana   Peru Medem   Luz Mejía   Jesús Mejías   Sonia Meléndez   Yael Meléndez   Miguel Ángel Mellado   Irene Méndez   Jean Méndez   Yokasta Mengó   Susana Mercado   Mariola Merino   Carmen Merlo   Ignacio Mery   Conchita Millán   Diego Minguet   Marcelo Miotto   Diego Miranda   Fernando Moiño   Carolina Montenegro   Alejandro Montero   Paloma Montero   Roberto Moraga   Pablo Moraleda   Pilar Morell   Ana Lisa Moreno   Esperanza Moreno   Esteban Moreno   Ester Moreno   Julio Moreno   Lourdes Moreno   Natalia Moreno   Sara Moreno   Lorena Moreta   María Mosquera   Victoria Munizaga   Paola Muñoz   María del Carmen Muriel   Eduardo Navarro   Manuel Navarro   Vicente Navarro   Pablo Navas   María Navascués   Anelusha Neacsu   Alejandro Nieto   Lindsay Nixon   Lara Nuevo   Vanessa Oleart   Óscar Olivares   Héctor Orden   Marco Orellana   Nicolás Orellana   Marco Ortega   María Ortega   Sara Ortega   Xell Orti   Gabriela Oscco   Miguel Oteo   Juan Antón Pacheco   Mariel Páez   Javier Palacios   David Palomares   Valentina Paredes   Jose Parejo   Roshan Patel   Carlos Peña   David Peña   Almudena Pérez   Bárbara Pérez   Cristina Pérez   David Pérez   Enrique Pérez   Jorge Pérez   Naira Pérez   Pepe Pérez   Sonia Pérez   César Pimentel   Paola Pineda   Marco Pino   Andrés Pinto   Felipe Pinto   Cecilia Piñeiro   Patrizia Plath   Eugenia Porras   Pedro Portillo   Luz Elena Pozzolungo   Geovanna Prado   Eduardo Prida   Ana Maria Prieto   Krzysztof Przybylo   Giovano Pulcioni   Adam Pyrek   Patricia Quilez   Hellmer Rahms   Florentino Ramírez   Javiera Ramírez   Paola Ramírez   Judith Ramón   Martina Rauhut   Javiera Riquelme   Martín Rivas   Carmen Rivero   Carlo Rizzi   Ben Robbins   Pierluca Roccheggiani   Isabel Rodrigo   Ángela Rodríguez   Cecilia Rodríguez   Gabriela Rodríguez   Joaquín Rodríguez   Johanna Rodríguez   Jorge Rodríguez   Manuel Rodríguez   Fabian Rogers   Daniela Rojas   Patricia Rojas   Fran Rojo   Irene Rojo   María Antonela Romano   Arturo Romero   Kevin Rosado   Raúl Rosado   Néstor Rouyet   Juan Manuel Rubio   Rudys Lane Rubio   Ángel Ruiz   Montserrat Ruiz   Daniela Saavedra   Claudia Sabán   Marta Sainz-Ezquerra   Masami Sakamoto   Elisabeth Salcedo   Leslie Salomón   Nicolás San Martín   Manuel San Miguel   Antonio Sánchez   Cristina Sánchez   Eduardo Sánchez   Enrique Sánchez   Fernando Sánchez   Isabel Sánchez   Jorge Sánchez   José Sánchez   Matías Sánchez   Santiago Sánchez   Manuel Sánchez de Ocaña   Laura Sancho   Francisco Sanjuán   Carlos Sanz   Reinaldo Sarmiento   Roberta Sartori   Susana Sastre   Wiktor Sawoch   Sebastian Schaub   Paola Seguel   Beatriz Sendín   Encarnación Serna   Teresa Serrano   Ana Serrano Mazo   Gabriel Sgorbini   Weynants Shawnee   Gentaro Shimada   Paz Sierra   Carla Silva   Christian Slaughter   Adriana Sobrini   David Sobrino   Marcos Souza   Ana Taboada de Zúñiga   Nicole Tauster   Alberto Tavera   Heide Taylor   Francisco José Terrero   Bárbara Tobar   Javier Torrado   Javier Torrecilla   Jose Antonio Torrecilla   Óscar Torrejón   Raúl Torres   Catalin Turian   Karissa Tyskilnd   Sol Uriarte   Ariel Urrea   Verónica van Kesteren   Daniela Vargas   Madelyn Vargas   Camila Vásquez   Luis Vásquez   Italo Veas   Jose Baúl Vega   Ana Vela   Marcos Velasco   Alfonso Velásquez   Manuel Vélez   Camila Vera   Marcos Viana   Luis Vidal   Miguel Ángel Vidal   Pablo Vila   Gorka Villaescusa   Mónica Villalba   Manuel Villanueva   Francisca Virán   Ana Visaires   Pablo Vives   Andrew Vuono   Nathaly Yamarte   Francisco Yáñez   Aldana Zabala   Darya Zhdanova   Li Ying Zheng

Credits

All graphic content in this book was created by Luis Vidal + Architects unless otherwise stated. Concept sketches by Luis Vidal; Illustrations by Nuria Campillo and Carlos Peña.

Palmas Altas Campus: Victor Sájara, pages 22–23, 28–29 by Mark Bentley; **Private House Renovation:** Ema Peter; **Heathrow Terminal 2:** courtesy of Heathrow Airport, pages 56, 57–58 by Andy Charlton, page 63: top by Andy Catterall, second line left Steve Bates, second line right Nick Wood, pages 60, 61, and bottom left on page 63 by James Newton; **Can Misses Hospital:** Ema Peter, page 70 by Xavi Duran; **Álvaro Cunqueiro Hospital:** Ema Peter; **Botín Center:** Enrico Cano; **Loyola University Campus:** Ema Peter, page 138 (top and bottom) and page 150 by Victor Sájara; **Castellana 77:** Fernando Andrés, page 163 courtesy of GMP; **Dallas-Fort Worth International Airport Terminal D Expansion:** Greg Folkins; **Matta Sur Community Centre & CESFAM:** Aryeh Kornfeld; **Arturo Merino Benítez International Airport Terminal 2:** Aryeh Kornfeld, pages 194–195, 207 courtesy of Nuevo Pudahuel; **Boston Logan International Airport Terminal E Modernization:** Ema Peter, page 211 by Pablo Vidal, page 214 by Luis Vidal; **New Colón Towers:** Ema Peter, pages 236–237 by Gorka Villaescusa, and pages 242–243 by Jose A. Quirantes Calvo; **Adolfo Suárez Madrid-Barajas Airport T4 & T4S Expansion and Modernization:** Luis Vidal + Architects, pages 248–249 by Ema Peter.

Palmas Altas Campus: Arup, Bovis, Calter; **Heathrow Terminal 2:** O.T. Ferrovial Agroman, Fhecor, Hoare Lea Consulting, Pascall + Watson (fit-out delivery team), Studio Fractal; **Can Misses Hospital:** Arup, CSP, D-fine; **Álvaro Cunqueiro Hospital:** Sven Dieter Adler, Arqui Lav, Calter, Idom ingenieria, Landelar, R7 Consultants; **Botín Center:** artec3 Studio, Arup, F. Caruncho, Dynamis, Gleeds, Müller BBM, PM Bovis, Typsa; **Loyola University Campus:** Calter Ingeniería, AAS Ermes Ingeniería de Instalaciones, Margarida Acústica, CSP; **Castellana 77:** Calter, Ineria, Vectoria; **Matta Sur Community Centre & CESFAM:** COBE, Estudio de Paisaje Arbolaria, José María Jiménez, One Geotecnia, Cristian Shaad; **Arturo Merino Benítez International Airport Terminal 2:** Arcadis, IDOM, Setec, VMB; **Boston Logan International Airport Terminal E Modernization:** Arora Engineers, BNP Associates, Rider Levett Bucknall, Code Red, Collaborative Lighting, Dharam Consulting, Ricondo, Thornton Tomasetti; **New Colón Towers:** Calter, Decibel, Krea, Liquid Ambar, Úrculo.

Book Coordinator: Ana Serrano Mazo

Director of Communications: Itziar de Francisco

CCO: Patricia Rojas

"My deepest gratitude to my team, clients, and everyone who contributes in making unexpected magic. And to my wife, Patricia, and our sons Javier, Pablo, and Marc, who bring the magic into my life."

—Luis Vidal

Published in Australia in 2024 by
The Images Publishing Group Pty Ltd
ABN 89 059 734 431

Offices

Melbourne
Waterman Business Centre
Suite 64, Level 2 UL40
1341 Dandenong Road
Chadstone, Victoria 3148
Australia
Tel: +61 3 8564 8122

New York
6 West 18th Street 4B
New York, NY 10011
United States
Tel: +1 212 645 1111

Shanghai
6F, Building C, 838 Guangji Road
Hongkou District, Shanghai 200434
China
Tel: +86 021 31260822

books@imagespublishing.com
www.imagespublishing.com

Copyright © Philip Jodidio (text) 2024; Luis Vidal + Architects 2024; and photographers as indicated 2024
The Images Publishing Group Reference Number: 1714

All photography is attributed on page 270 unless otherwise noted.
Cover: Ema Peter (Luis Vidal + Architects, Boston Logan International Airport Terminal E Modernization)

All rights reserved. Apart from any fair dealing for the purposes of private study, research, criticism or review as permitted under the Copyright Act, no part of this publication may be reproduced, stored in a retrieval system, or transmitted in any form by any means, electronic, mechanical, photocopying, recording or otherwise, without the written permission of the publisher.

A catalogue record for this book is available from the National Library of Australia

Title: Luis Vidal + Architects: Expect the Unexpected // edited by Philip Jodidio
ISBN: 9781864709841

This title was commissioned in IMAGES' Melbourne office and produced as follows:
Editorial Georgia (Gina) Tsarouhas, Rebecca Gross *Art direction/production* Nicole Boehringer

Printed by O.G.M. SpA, Padova, Italy, on 150gsm Gardamatt art paper

IMAGES has included on its website a page for special notices in relation to this and its other publications.
Please visit www.imagespublishing.com

Every effort has been made to trace the original source of copyright material contained in this book.
The publishers would be pleased to hear from copyright holders to rectify any errors or omissions.
The information and illustrations in this publication have been prepared and supplied by Luis Vidal + Architects, Philip Jodidio, and the participants. While all reasonable efforts have been made to ensure accuracy, the publishers do not, under any circumstances, accept responsibility for errors, omissions and representations express or implied.